Journaling

from the Heart

A Writing Workshop
in Three Parts

Eldonna Edwards Bouton

www.whole-heart.com

ATTENTION JOURNALING WORKSHOPS, HEALING CENTERS, ORGANIZATIONS, AND SCHOOLS OF SPIRITUAL DEVELOPMENT: Quantity discounts available on bulk purchases of this book for educational purposes or for fundraising. For information, contact the publisher at the address below.

Whole Heart Publications
P.O. Box 14358
San Luis Obispo, CA
93406-4358

Phone/Fax: 805-543-8640
E-mail: info@whole-heart.com
http://www.whole-heart.com

Manufactured in the USA

ISBN 0-0967384-1-3

Cover design by Debra O'Brien Star (debra@slonet.org)

Other books by Eldonna Edwards Bouton:

Loose Ends, A Journaling Tool for Tying up the Incomplete Details of your Life and Heart, ISBN# 0967038405

Write Away: A Journal Writing Toolkit, 0976038421

See back page for ordering information

Dedication

This is for each of you who have come to the journal to face your fears, reclaim your spirit, and dream upon the page.

From my ♥
to yours!

Donna Elmer Bond

"Talking to the paper is like talking to the Divine. Paper is infinitely patient. Each time you scratch on it, you trace part of yourself, and thus part of the world, and thus part of the grammar of the universe. It is a huge language, but each of us tracks his or her particular understanding of it."

Burghild Nina Holzer
A Walk Between Heaven and Earth

Table of Contents

Acknowledgements

I remain humbly grateful to the following people who have supported me in a multitude of ways over the course of bringing this book from thought to workshop to print: All the beautiful people from Scribe Tribe/Journal Joy/Journal Women/Spiral Journey/Journal Writing and my own Writefully-Yours e-lists, Journaling from the Heart workshop participants, A Woman's Write retreat participants, Kay Adams from the Center for Journal Therapy, Catherine de Cuir of aboutjournals.com, Lael Johnson and the members of the National Journal Network, lisa schumicky (diarist extraordinaire), Debra O'Brien, Micheala O'Connor, Jan Forrest, my fellow CCAMC buddies, Linda Margison, David Congalton, Todd & Sage Tyrtle, and all those who have purchased my books and services. Special thanks to my husband Bill for his patience and support and my son Jacob for loving me unconditionally, even if that means having Mom at her computer when he'd rather play Monopoly.

And to the Magnificent Muse who continues to whisper in my ear.

Introduction

If you bought this book, then you probably don't need me to convince you of the many therapeutic benefits of journaling. There are a lot of journaling books out there, many of which I have included in the bibliography. So what makes this book different?

As an author and journaling workshop facilitator, I have discovered that there are three basic reasons people use the written word as a pathway to their souls.

1. To reconnect with the lost self.
2. To create the life they crave.
3. To tap into their creativity.

Quite often a person will come to the journal with the first reason in mind, then gradually develop a desire for the second two reasons. This is easy to understand. Once you have gathered up the lost parts of yourself and identified behaviors that no longer suit you, the next obvious step is to want to redefine your life. By recording your dreams and passions, you are on your way to creating the life you desire. And finally, because journaling taps into the creative well within each of us, many of you will begin to be more creative in your journals.

Although the first step can be the most challenging, the rewards of reclaiming your spirit and recognizing the lost parts of yourself as they appear on the page, can also be exhilarating.

In 1999, I developed three separate journaling workshops based upon the specific goals outlined above, which I taught both in face-to-face groups and on the Internet. As a result of the success of these workshops, I decided that anyone who desires to participate in this program should have access to the exercises. You can use this book to complete the workshops independently in the privacy of your home, or to form a journaling support group-workshop in your community. Information on how to form a Journaling from the Heart™ workshop in your area follows this Introduction.

This book is designed to offer gentle prompts to help you to achieve your journaling goals. Although you do not have to complete the workshops in chronological order, I strongly recommend it to achieve the most benefit.

There are no rules in journaling, however, here are a few guidelines to keep in mind:

1. Make a commitment to the workshop. I call the exercises "assignments" because if you are here to do the work, then you need to show up. If you find yourself resisting an exercise, ask yourself why. Is it because you have already done the work (fine, then skip ahead to the next one) or is it because this is an issue that you really need to work through? If so, take a deep breath and dive in.

2. Do your writing when you have quiet, uninterrupted space. We'll discuss how to create that space early on in Workshop One. Also, don't negotiate away your writing time. Embrace it, demand it, and cherish it.

3. If you run into trouble GET HELP. This workshop is designed to help you find yourself. Sometimes you will find things that have been hiding for a long time, and some of those things may be very painful. Although journaling is a

great adjunct to therapy, it cannot take the place of professional help.

4. Be gentle with yourself. Kick the editor, the parent, and the critic out of the room when you write. Don't judge or correct yourself as you write. Keep your pen to the page and just keep writing.

5. Have fun. Some of these exercises are serious, but the ultimate goal is to experience joy. Learn to laugh at yourself. Play with the exercises. Ask yourself, "Will this be funny later?" If so, then let it be funny now. If not, then ask whether or not it will be important twenty or ten or even one year from now. In this way you can remain more objective through those writings that may leave you feeling tired, frustrated, or scared.

I hope that you find working through these workshops as fulfilling as I have in creating and facilitating them. I look forward to hearing from you on the success of your journaling journey. If there's any ink left in your pen, write me a letter or e-mail me. I love getting mail.

Writefully Yours,

Eldonna Edwards Bouton

How to form a Journaling Group

Although journaling is a private journey, it is sometimes helpful to have others bear witness to your progress. A journaling group offers support, motivation, and accountability. If done mindfully, you can create a circle of journalers where each participant feels safe, supported, and valuable.

The exercises in this book are designed to be completed as daily (weekday) assignments. Your group can come together once a week to reflect and share the week's work, read portions of their writings, or choose one particular assignment each week to share. At this pace, each workshop will run for approximately one month or a total of three months if you remain grouped for all three workshops.

You can also form a long-term journaling group where you each work one exercise per week, in which case it will take seventy-five weeks to complete the entire book. Imagine the bond you will form doing this work together for a year and a half!

Here are some guidelines for you to follow when working through the exercises in this book as a group.

1. Choose your participants carefully. Be sure that whoever you accept into your group is committed to showing up and understands the importance of privacy.

2. Limit your group to five or six so that everyone who chooses to has the opportunity to read.

3. Respect the choice of any individual NOT to read.

4. Take turns "facilitating" each session so that one person does not have to do all the prep work (such as snacks, meeting place, etc.)

5. Be a witness to your fellow journalers. Do not judge or criticize what someone has shared. Offer gentle support rather than advice.

6. Never repeat anything shared in the workshop.

7. Create an opening and closing ritual to emphasize entry into the group's intention and closure of each session. This will help to maintain focus and move the dynamic from "chat" mode to journaling mode. In my workshops I like to light a candle at the beginning of each session to remind us that we are all gathered to share a common fire. I close with a selected piece of music so that everyone has a chance to quietly reflect and integrate what has been learned/shared. Of course, because I happen to be a tactile person, nobody gets away without a hug.

We offer group discounts, by the way, to groups ordering five or more books for the purpose of forming a journaling workshop. Call Whole Heart Publications at 805-543-8640 for more information.

Journaling from the Heart

A Writing Workshop in Three Parts

Workshop One

Introduction to Journaling
&
Reconnecting with the Lost Self

Introduction to Part One

In this workshop, you will be given exercises to lead you on a journey to reclaim the lost parts of yourself, face your fears, identify patterns of behavior that no longer serve you, and to help you let go of your attachment to the past. The goal is to once again become familiar with who you are and what you want.

Although some of these exercises may feel "dark" or "heavy" it is my belief that until you are able to not only acknowledge but embrace the darkness, you will be unable to walk fully into the light.

Think of this portion of the workshop as a river. You wade into the water, swim a little, dive deeper from time to time, and surface on the far shore lighter and stronger. Sometimes it may feel as if you are swimming upstream, but this is usually only the occasional rapids you are treading. Hold on tight and keep an eye on the shore.

Journaling is a pathway to the soul. Let your words light the way. Let your thoughts be free. Let your heart be honest.

(Record your mood going into the exercise)

Choosing the Tools

The tools we use say a lot about who we are. It is important for you choose a journal that feels good in your hands. Even though you may be posting your entries into a computer, I encourage you to write in longhand first. There is a definite benefit in the kinesthetic release of writing that which is in your heart, by allowing it to travel down your arm and out of your fingers as you form each letter.

Your first assignment is to choose a special journal for this workshop. Take some time to visit your local art or office supply store and select a journal that feels good in your hands. Better yet, let your journal choose you. Do you prefer lines or no lines? Hardbound or spiral? Play with pens. Would a fountain pen inspire you? Have you tried the sparkly gel pens? Even if you end up with a legal pad and a pencil, the point is that you find what will be the most comfortable for you to use.

When you get home, personalize your Workshop Journal. Cut out a picture that represents who you are right now. Maybe who you are is a tree, or a rock or a cat. That's okay. Or find a photo of yourself and paste it on the cover or inside the first page. You may even choose a photo of your child self. Or draw a picture. Or write a quote that speaks to you. Then, date the first page.

Write: "Dear Journal: What I want from you is..."

Don't edit yourself as you write. Keep your pen to the paper and just write what comes out, even if it ends up being something other than what you had planned.

Upon completion, reflect:

· How did this go for me?
· What did I learn?
· This brought up something new (what?)

(Record your mood after completing the exercise.)

Part One
Assignment #2

(Record your mood going into the exercise)

Your Sanctuary

When I was a little girl I used to go into the closet of the bedroom I shared with my sister and sit on the shelf over the heating duct. It seemed like a huge space at the time, but I expect if I were to revisit it today, I would wonder how I found comfort there. Yet I did then because it was my private place and it brought me peace. In the winter especially, I liked how the heat flowed beneath me-as if it ran through me-and warmed me from the inside out. I even talked to invisible friends there in the closet; the ones who lived within the ductwork. But that's another story.

Today's assignment is to write about your favorite place to write. Describe this place using all your senses. Do you have a view? Are you surrounded by your favorite things? What are they? If not, fill your space with items that inspire and comfort you. I encourage you to learn to write wherever you are, but to also have a place, a sacred space, where you write on a regular basis. In this place you will come to find your heart wide open and willing to share.

Upon completion, reflect:

- How did this go for me?
- What did I learn?
- This brought up something new (what?)

(Record your mood after completing the exercise.)

Part One
Assignment #3

(Record your mood going into the exercise)

A Time to Write

"I don't have time!"

If I had a dime for every time I heard this excuse for not writing, I wouldn't have to worry about paying off my second mortgage. In a society where people try to cram a week's worth of activity into a day, it is no wonder that time has become such a precious commodity.

However, in order for your journal writing practice to be successful, you MUST make the time to write. In fact, it has been shown that by writing at the same time every day over a period of about three weeks, one will establish a habit wherein the urge to write at the specified time of day will occur.

Your next assignment is to write a contract between yourself and your journal. Turn off the television, skip the newspaper, do whatever it takes to create your journaling time. Demand it of yourself and of those around you.

Date your entry. Write, "I promise to write every day for at least twenty minutes at _____." Sign it.

I am a strong believer in symbolism. It may help to actually draw a clock on the page with the hands set at your optimum writing time. Or write the time in large numbers and color it in. For example, I like to write at dawn, so I drew a sun rising over my page.

Upon completion, reflect:

· How did this go for me?
· What did I learn?
· This brought up something new (what?)

(Record your mood after completing the exercise.)

Part One
Assignment #4

(Record your mood going into the exercise)

Who Am I?

Depending upon who is doing the asking, I might answer this question in several ways:

1. I'm someone's mother
2. I'm someone's writing coach
3. I'm someone's therapist
4. I'm someone's friend

Notice that each of these answers is based upon my relationship to others. We all have important roles that we fill, however, the point of this exercise is to find who you are at your core. Too often, we give away pieces of ourselves in exchange for the parts we play. For instance, by choosing motherhood, perhaps you gave up dancing, thinking it frivolous in relation to your responsibility as a mother. Or maybe you have put off a lifelong desire (such as going back to school or being a writer) because it didn't fit with your other roles.

In this assignment, you will list who you are, the part that you may not share with everyone else, as well as the roles you play. For example:

I am a Buddhist
I am a lover
I am an aunt
I am a dreamer
I am a writer
I am a dancer
I am a survivor
I am bloated
I am imperfect
I am needy
I am strong

See what happened here? This list went from what to who. Who you are does not necessarily have to be a noun. You may be silly. Who you are may be a metaphor, such as a whisper or a dance. Do not be confined by what makes sense. If you write, "I am purple" that just means that you feel purple today. Start a list of who you are. Do not edit yourself. The longer you go the deeper you will reach into the core of who you are.

Upon completion, reflect:

· How did this go for me?
· What did I learn?
· This brought up something new (what?)

(Record your mood after completing the exercise.)

Part One
Assignment #5

(Record your mood going into the exercise.)

Relationship to Self

If only we were as good to ourselves as we are to others. Take a look at your list from assignment #4. Choose those words that would be defined as based upon your relationship to others; words like mother, wife, brother, boss, employee, friend, etc. Think about your relationship to yourself. Do you treat yourself as well as you treat others? Do you give yourself adequate vacation time and bonuses (employer)? Do you treat yourself tenderly when you're not feeling well (parent)? Do you put forth your best effort in order to be good at whatever it is you strive to be (employee)? Do you love yourself unconditionally (child)? Are you always "there" for yourself in difficult times (friend)? Are you your own greatest advocate (partner)? Do you even treat yourself as well as your pets?

Write about your relationship with yourself. Write honestly and deeply. Let the writing sit for a while, then go back and reread your entry. Add another entry in which you promise yourself to improve those areas that need work. Be specific. For instance, you may write, "I will allow myself to take a nap when I'm feeling tired. " Or, "I will give myself a trip to the museum or a dinner out just because I deserve it."

Upon completion, reflect:

- How did this go for me?
- What did I learn?
- This brought up something new (what?)

(Record your mood after completing the exercise.)

Part One
Assignment #6

(Record your mood going into the exercise.)

The Shadow Knows

When you were a child, were you afraid to dangle your arms or legs over the side of the bed for fear of what awful unknown thing might be lying in wait? Did you have a night light in your room? Did the toys on the dresser become monsters within the darkness?

Most of us are afraid of the dark, even if just a little bit. It is not because we know that some terrible creature is lurking in the shadows, but the unknown that frightens us.

As human beings, we often avoid the shadowy side of our beings as well. But it is important to acknowledge all facets of ourselves, dark as well as light, in order to become fully authentic. Even if that means admitting to the parts of us we're not very proud of; the part of us that tells lies, judges others, screams at our kids when we lose control, or eats too much. It is important to be aware of the totality of who we are.

Please do not use this exercise to beat yourself up. The purpose of this assignment is to become more comfortable with the whole you. Write about your dark side. Write freely and

15

honestly. Try to just "notice" these parts of yourself rather than judge them. Make a list. Hint: Often what really bugs you about other people is something they are mirroring from your shadow side. For instance, I abhor cigarette smoke. Guess who used to smoke? It is my own tendency toward a lack of discipline that causes me to get uptight about smoking. Here is a sample list from an anonymous journaler:

I pee in the shower.
I eat when I am hungry for love.
I am attracted to people of my own sex.
I fake orgasms.
I drink too much alcohol.
I sometimes want to kick my dog

These are brave and honest entries. It doesn't mean that this person is bad. It just means that she is willing to look at all sides of herself. Take some deep breaths. Remember not to judge yourself as you write.

Upon completion, reflect:

· How did this go for me?
· What did I learn?
· This brought up something new (what?)

(Record your mood after completing the exercise.)

Part One
Assignment #7

(Record your mood going into the exercise.)

Popping the Question

Often we turn to the journal looking for answers. Sometimes the answers appear in the form of more questions. For instance, I may ask my journal, "Why can't I seem to stick with an exercise program?" My next sentence might be "What if I don't really like going to the gym? What if there is some other form of exercise that works better for me? What if I bicycled or walked instead?"

As you can see, I answered each question with another question which in my case, led to a discovery of why I was using avoidance and procrastination to sabotage a plan that wasn't right for me.

In today's assignment you are to only write questions. Ask away, varying your questions with what, what if, where, why, when and how. Try not to plan what you're going to ask, but rather let the questions tumble forth organically. Many of your questions will spontaneously give birth to other questions. Keep writing until you feel as if you have come to some sort of conclusion to a theme.

Upon completion, reflect:

· How did this go for me?
· What did I learn?
· This brought up something new (what?)

(Record your mood after completing the exercise.)

(Record your mood going into the exercise.)

Answering Machine 12/20/04

In many ways we are like answering machines, recording messages and relaying them to other parts of our being.

"Hi, this is me. Please leave a message after the beep."

"Beeeeep. Its me, your ego, just letting you know I'm craving some attention. How about taking me out in that new outfit or calling you-know-who to brag about you-know what."

"Beeeeep. Oh hi, it's your intuition here reminding you that you can trust me."

"Beeeeep. Hello? This is your sex drive. We haven't been doing much driving lately if you know what I mean. Do you think we could go for a ride soon?"

"Beeeeep. Um, this is your inner child and um I was wondering if maybe we could go play for a while? I kinda want to build a fort in the living room but I'll settle for a bubble bath and some popcorn, 'kay? And can we please use purple in the journal today?"

"Beeeeep. Hey! Ignore all your other calls. This is your soul and I need to be fed RIGHT NOW! Please go find your journal and do some writing so I can share more."

Okay, so I'm keeping it light, but hopefully you're getting the message. More importantly, I hope you are getting YOUR messages. Go back and look at your list of questions from assignment #7. Now connect with your inner message center and start writing the answers. Be sure to check in with your body, mind and spirit selves.

Upon completion, reflect:

· How did this go for me?
· What did I learn?
· This brought up something new (what?)

(Record your mood after completing the exercise.)

Part One
Assignment #9

(Record your mood going into the exercise.)

What's Bugging You? 12/13/04

Have you ever noticed how extremely people sometimes react to the most minor infractions? Road rage is a perfect example. Someone pulls out in front of you and instead of slowing down, you speed up just to show them whose boss, scowl, curse, maybe even give them the finger. Okay maybe you or I wouldn't do this, but a lot of people do and even go so far as to use a gun to confront that evil driver.

Maybe you snap at someone you love, treat a customer with impatience, or show your intolerance of another's stupidity by making a vicious remark. Usually when we find ourselves flinging darts at others, it is not about the situation at hand. Usually, the anger or frustration runs much deeper and is much older than today.

In this exercise you will write down a sentence that defines something that's bugging you. Then, ask yourself, "What's under that?" Write the next sentence. Repeat, "What's under that?" Keep going until you feel you've gotten to the root of the problem. Here is an example:

Problem: My partner doesn't pay attention to me. (What's under that?)
I'm angry because I'm not important to him. (W.U.T.?)
I need more attention. (W.U.T.?)
I feel insignificant. (W.U.T.?)
I wish I were important to him. (W.U.T.?)
I feel unimportant. (W.U.T.?)
Important people matter. (W.U.T.?)
I don't matter. (W.U.T.?)
I've never mattered. (W.U.T.?)
I felt invisible as a child. (W.U.T.?)
I wanted attention from my parents and teachers and schoolmates. (W.U.T.?)
I wanted to matter. (W.U.T.?)
I wanted love. (W.U.T.?)
Attention=Love. (W.U.T.?)
I want to be loved. (W.U.T.?)

Realization: I don't love myself.
Solution: If I love myself others will love me also.

(Special thanks to Su Bibik at The Kalamazoo Center for the Healing Arts for turning me on to this wonderfully effective exercise.)

Upon completion, reflect:

· How did this go for me?
· What did I learn?
· This brought up something new (what?)

(Record your mood after completing the exercise.)

Part One
Assignment #10

(Record your mood going into the exercise.)

Revisiting the Shadow

In assignment #6 we took a peek into the shadows to see what might be lurking there. I'm betting you may have uncovered a few skeletons that you'd just as soon were decomposed. I've left your bones to sit for a while to give you a chance to integrate whatever may have come up for you in that exercise. Today it is time to revisit that place where you hold the truth of all sides of you.

Go back and take a look at your entry from Assignment #6. Read through the descriptions of your shadow side. Then ask yourself the following three questions:

1. Which of these things about myself would I like to change?
2. Which ones am I willing to change?
3. What steps can I take to change these things?

Be mindful as you write the answers. Don't flog yourself. Instead, acknowledge yourself for being willing to make courageous leaps toward becoming the best person you can be.

Here is an example from our anonymous journaler in Assignment #6:

2.A) I'd like to learn to better control my temper.

2.B) I want be authentic with my lover.

3.A) I will breathe slowly and count from ten to one when I feel myself losing control. I will go for a walk if I feel like I cannot control my temper. I will journal about those things that are my temper triggers in an attempt to isolate them.

3.B) I will ask for what I need from my lover. I will say no when I don't feel like having sex. I will be true to myself always and in all ways.

Hint: Keep these in the positive voice. (Use "I will" instead of "I won't.")

Upon completion, reflect:

· How did this go for me?
· What did I learn?
· This brought up something new (what?)

(Record your mood after completing the exercise.)

Part One
Assignment #11

(Record your mood going into the exercise.)

Tearing Down the Walls

Sometimes no matter how sincere our intentions are to overcome stumbling blocks, we keep slamming into the same old walls. Perhaps you've promised not to allow yourself to let so-and-so push your buttons ever again. And yet when you think of this person your stomach still does a hideous flip and you know in your heart that you are not finished with this one yet. But what do you do?

Forgive. Not in the way most people think of forgiving-as letting someone off the hook for something they've done-but as letting go. Or putting it another way, removing yourself from the other person's hook so that they no longer have power over your emotions.

Is there someone or something that is blocking your path to wholeness? Does this person or thing keep you from being fully present because you still have one foot firmly planted in the past? Has the dynamic associated with this situation become miserably familiar and tiresome? Are you ready to sincerely let go?

In this exercise you will identify a thing, person, or relationship that is keeping you segmented and unable to move forward. Write about it one last time. Go ahead and spill your guts, whine, cry, swear, and scream if you like. Do not read any further until you have finished this part.

Now, begin on a fresh page. Write, "I am ready to let go of what no longer serves me. I forgive myself for my part in _____ and I release _____ for his/her/its power over my life. I will no longer waste any more precious energy on _____ and I bless _____ with all the good I want returned to me.

If any of these words hold negative images for you, choose your own phrasing. What is important is that you write about what is blocking you on your path to wholeness and then let go of it.

Upon completion, reflect:

· How did this go for me?
· What did I learn?
· This brought up something new (what?)

(Record your mood after completing the exercise.)

Part One
Assignment #12

(Record your mood going into the exercise.)

If Only

"If only I had finished college, then I would have a better job."
"If only I could leave my husband, then I'd be happier."
"If only I had more money..."
"If only I were prettier..."
"If only I had a bigger house (nicer car, better clothes...)"

Do any of these lines sound familiar? Do you have a litany of "if only's" you rattle off as excuses for not being happy or living up to your potential? No? Then take the day off and celebrate your ability to create the life you want. The other 98% of us have some work to do.

Recently I told myself, "If only I had a walking partner I would be able to be get exercise." I know that I feel better when I walk regularly, yet I consistently used the lack of someone to walk with as a reason for not getting out there and trekking for forty-five minutes a day. I finally had to admit to myself that it wasn't a lack of a walking partner that was holding me back. It was a lack of motivation and nobody was to blame but me. I'd fallen out of the habit and it was up to me to recreate the habit.

Because my body and its health are priorities, I designed an exercise to combat my self-sabotage. For every "if only" I wrote, 'This is important to me so I will_____ in order to make _____ happen." Through this exercise I found ways to dissolve my old excuses. I bought a micro-cassette recorder so that I could "write" while walking, I decided to walk in the afternoon when it was warmer, and I began getting up earlier in the morning to have more time to write.

Write out your list of "If only's." Follow-up with a list of your priorities, based upon what you are being kept from (financial abundance, security, happiness, good health, etc.). Then arm yourself with your pen and deactivate your excuses with ways to create the life you desire.

Upon completion, reflect:

· How did this go for me?
· What did I learn?
· This brought up something new (what?)

(Record your mood after completing the exercise.)

Part One
Assignment #13

(Record your mood going into the exercise.)

Operating Instructions

Have you ever said or done something and had your spouse or your child look at you as if you were from another planet? Have you ever had someone ask you a question that you've answered a million times but they just can't seem to remember it? And what of new relationships? Wouldn't it be wonderful if we could hand our lover a little booklet and say, 'Read this. Call me when you've studied it. There'll be a test later."

How wonderful it would be if our children, friends, lovers, and families all came with an owner's manual! Just think. The next time your main squeeze hints about Friday night, you could say, "Page 17. This model likes dramas, documentaries, and dark comedy. No shoot-em-ups or slapstick. Bonus points for chick-flicks."

In this exercise you will write an owners manual for yourself. You can write it generically or for a specific "owner" such as a spouse, parent, or friend. Be specific. Here's an excerpt from one I wrote for my husband:

She likes flowers but would rather have them growing outside her window than in a vase. If you want romance, begin foreplay with kindness throughout the day. Bring her chocolate when she's moody. Dark chocolate. Tell her often that you love her. Tell her why. Assume she's as intelligent as you are (or more). Treat her as you would a priceless gem. She is. Give her freedom to continue to grow. Applaud her accomplishments. Hold her. A lot. Rub her feet when she's tired. And get rid of the photos of old girlfriends. She's your history now.

Here's your chance to give others your own personal set of operating instructions. Feel free to keep adding to this one later as you think of more.

Optional Exercise: Write an owner's manual for someone you love. Ask them to write one for you. Exchange them. Voila'! No excuses.

Upon completion, reflect:

· How did this go for me?
· What did I learn?
· This brought up something new (what?)

(Record your mood after completing the exercise.)

Part One
Assignment #14

(Record your mood going into the exercise.)

The Best Things in Life

Beaches
Cuddling
Sunsets
Sunrises
Chocolate
Summer rain
The smell of coffee brewing first thing in the morning
Kissing baby feet
Dancing wildly
Making mad passionate love...in a meadow
Butterflies
Hearing "I love you"
Did I mention chocolate?
Cotton jammies
Listening to a favorite CD
Bumming around in an art supply store
Sipping a smoothie (or sucking it down)
Coloring
Going to the Drive-In

These are just a few of the things that make life worth living for me. Some of life's simplest pleasures are the ones that still take my breath away. Yet so often I forget, get caught up in life's little miseries. That's when I need to haul out my list.

In this exercise you will make a list of all the best things in life. Blend a lot of free things in with the ones that cost money. Then choose at least one thing from your list and DO IT. Spend your lunch hour at the art museum (or at the hardware store). Bring your favorite sandwich to work. Buy flowers and put them on your desk. Call someone you love.

Make a copy of your list and put it in your purse or your wallet. The next time you're feeling down, take out your list and find something there that will bring a smile back to your face. Remind yourself of the abundant pleasures you have available to you. Continue to fill your life with things from your list. Add more items as you think of them.

Upon completion, reflect:

· How did this go for me?
· What did I learn?
· This brought up something new (what?)

(Record your mood after completing the exercise.)

Part One
Assignment #15

(Record your mood going into the exercise.)

Mystery Date

How long has it been since you've done something that you really wanted to do? Do you even give yourself permission to indulge your inner yearnings? Do you deny yourself a tasty treat from time to time (ice-cream is too fattening) or a movie (I'll wait for the video/watch what others want to watch) or a dinner out (a waste of money) or a massage (too frivolous)?

assignment for 1/31/05

Well today you not only have permission to do something nice for yourself, it is your assignment. In the next 48 hours you are to choose something you would not normally indulge your-self in such as an item from the previous exercise or some-thing else you rarely allow yourself. Whatever you do, choose willingly and without hesitation. Be extravagant. That doesn't have to mean an expensive gift or outing, it just means to do it up right. Order two scoops. Schedule an hour and a half mas-sage. See a double feature with popcorn and Goobers.

Afterwards, write about how it felt to give in to self-pleasure. Were you able to do it guiltlessly? What feelings came up? Do you tend toward a life of scarcity; believing there's not enough to go around? Or did you fully engage yourself in the pleasure

33

of a little indulgence? It is important to nurture yourself on a regular basis. Self-care is required for healthy body/mind/spirit well being. You deserve it.

Upon completion, reflect:

· How did this go for me?
· What did I learn?
· This brought up something new (what?)

(Record your mood after completing the exercise.)

Part One
Assignment #16

(Record your mood going into the exercise.)

Miracles

I've never been able to walk on water or for that matter seen anyone else do it, but I do know a miracle when I see one. For instance, when my son was nearly two, he disappeared from my sight. The next several minutes seemed to stretch out over eternity, in slow motion. When I called for my son he didn't answer. My thirteen year-old daughter and I searched high and low for him. No Jacob. My stomach did an ugly drop as I ran to the back door off the kitchen. Sure enough, someone had left it unlatched when they'd gone out.

At that time we had a pool in our back yard. It was late fall and the pool was covered with black plastic, which was by this time full of dead leaves. The thought of my baby in that cold dark water made me physically ill. I pawed at the plastic and screamed for help. The water beneath the cover was nearly as black as the cover.

With tears running down my face and my heart leaping out of my chest, I turned to see an angel; my daughter, carrying a grinning Jacob. She'd found him hiding in an upstairs closet.

The rush of love that ran through my veins was enough to fill that pool. I knew that I had been handed a miracle. The house went up for sale the next week and we moved to a more childproof home.

Write about the miracles in your life. Consider how blessed you are.

Upon completion, reflect:

· How did this go for me?
· What did I learn?
· This brought up something new (what?)

(Record your mood after completing the exercise.)

Part One
Assignment #17

(Record your mood going into the exercise.)

Shameless

From the time we are born, most of us are bombarded with shaming messages from parents, the church, and even our partners. As time wears on, these messages get imprinted on a deeper and deeper level. Often, even as we try to break out of old patterns, the old tapes kick in and begin playing their outmoded tunes.

Today's exercise seeks to release those shaming messages. One by one you will reach down, pull out a tape, and then write over it. If you are a computer person, think of it as reformatting old disks. We are going to erase the outdated and limiting data and replace it with permission and acceptance. At the top of your page write, "IT IS OKAY TO" and then start your list. Here is an example:

IT IS OKAY TO:

Not make my bed every day
Jump on the bed
Eat in bed if I want to
Stay up late

Sleep in if I need it
Call in sick when I am ill
Not answer the phone
Have an occasional fattening treat
Read a trashy novel
Feed the kids macaroni & cheese when I'm tired
Be angry
Cry
Feel sad
Have a different opinion
Not eat every thing on my plate
Say no

Upon completion, reflect:

· How did this go for me?
· What did I learn?
· This brought up something new (what?)

(Record your mood after completing the exercise.)

Part One
Assignment #18

(Record your mood going into the exercise.)

Lost and Found

The other day I found a piece of paper containing the lyrics to a song I had once written. I never finished the song, but reading those lyrics made me remember a time in my life when I thought I had lost my way.

There is so much we have lost in our lives, both literally and metaphorically. In Part One of today's exercise, you will write a list of things you have lost. Keep your pen to the page and keep writing for as long as you can. Here is a sample list:

What I Have Lost:

My baby teeth
One of my favorite earrings
My innocence
My virginity
My early journals
$30 somewhere between school and home
A mother
My youth (some of it)

My fear of speaking in public
15 pounds (found five of them)

Get the idea? Okay, make your list. Then, in Part Two of this exercise, choose one thing on the list and write about it. If you knew where it was, where would it be? Do you still want it back? Do you miss it?

Upon completion, reflect:

- How did this go for me?
- What did I learn?
- This brought up something new (what?)

(Record your mood after completing the exercise.)

(Record your mood going into the exercise.)

Mission Accomplished

One does not go through life without wondering why they are here from time to time. If it weren't for this inherent need for purpose, I doubt religions would exist in their current form. We all want to know what our mission is.

Even if you have not figured out the meaning of life, you can and do have a say in your intentions. What I mean by this is that just as companies publish a public mission statement to disclose their corporate intention, so can you create your own personal mission statement. You can state to the world (and to yourself) what your mission is as a reminder of why you are here at this very moment, and what you trying to accomplish. Here is an example of my Personal Mission Statement:

Eldonna exists to find meaning in both the joy and the sadness that life offers. She fully intends to celebrate life by offering loving reciprocity to those who have blessed her with their presence, the earth that nourishes her, and the body that supports her existence. She lives by a code of gentle-kindness and compassion. Eldonna accepts the responsibilities of healing touch and creative expression through words and music.

41

When you write your mission statement, keep in mind that this is your present intention. Your mission statement may change as you grow and change. You can also write categorical mission statements, such as one for your career, your primary relationships, or your spiritual quest. It's very exciting to write a marital mission statement together with your partner.

Upon completion, reflect:

· How did this go for me?
· What did I learn?
· This brought up something new (what?)

(Record your mood after completing the exercise.)

Part One
Assignment #20

(Record your mood going into the exercise.)

My Body, Myself: Part One

Remember when you were a child and you never wondered how your butt looked from behind or thought twice about what you put in your mouth, as long as it tasted good?

Our bodies are so forgiving of what we do to them. Yet, if we were to take a moment to listen to our bodies both when they are jumping up and down with pleasure and when they are screaming in pain, we might be able to learn something from what the body is trying to tell us.

On a blank piece of paper, draw a picture of your body. Use red to highlight the areas that are needy or in pain. Pay attention to the messages your body is giving you. It doesn't have to be a detailed picture. It can even be a stick drawing.

Next, sit down and let your body write a letter to you. Let your body complain about the way you sometimes treat it, tell you what it enjoys and needs the most, and thank you for the wonderful ways you often show your love for it. Bodies don't judge. They just want to support you. Listen to your body.

Upon completion, reflect:

· How did this go for me?
· What did I learn?
· This brought up something new (what?)

(Record your mood after completing the exercise.)

Part One
Assignment #21

(Record your mood going into the exercise.)

My Body, Myself: Part Two

In the previous exercise you let your body write you a letter to ask for what it needs. Something you may have found is that the body is very direct in making its needs known.

Today you will write a letter back to your body, promising to care for it.

First, find a picture (or draw one) of yourself. Paste it into your journal. Then write Dear _____ (your name). As you write this letter, forgive yourself for anything you've done to abuse or neglect your body in the past.

Afterwards, make a list of things you can do to create more perfect health for yourself nutritionally, aerobically, and just for pleasure. Copy the list under your picture.

Your body is sacred. Offer it many gifts. You will be amply rewarded.

Upon completion, reflect:

- How did this go for me?
- What did I learn?
- This brought up something new (what?)

(Record your mood after completing the exercise.)

Part One
Assignment #22

(Record your mood going into the exercise.)

Inner Wisdom

Have you ever been stressed out about a relatively small thing, only to realize after it was over how insignificant that one thing was in the Big Picture? Was the argument over which wallpaper to use in the bathroom, really that important? Did anyone even notice that you were having a bad hair day yesterday?

Imagine for a moment that you are sitting on a porch swing, perhaps holding a glass of lemonade. Next to you, in your favorite rocker, sits your ninety-year-old self. He or she is there to answer any questions you may have about your life.

Ask your Wise Self what was most important in this life. Ask any question you may have.

Listen quietly to the answers and write them down in your journal. In this way you can come to an understanding of what is most important to you in this lifetime. Ask what you most regret doing, or more importantly, regret not doing.

Upon completion, reflect:

· How did this go for me?
· What did I learn?
· This brought up something new (what?)

(Record your mood after completing the exercise.)

Part One
Assignment #23

(Record your mood going into the exercise.)

Daily Inventory

As you near completion of Workshop One, you may be thinking, "Well yeah, it was fine as long as I had these assignments to work with. But what if I can't think of anything to journal about on my own?"

Today you're going to negate that excuse. Here's how.

On a sheet of paper or somewhere in your journal that you can tag for easy reference, write the numbers 1 through 31. After each number write a word or phrase that represents a thing, person, situation or emotion that you would like to keep tabs on. Here is a sample from my list.

1. social activities
2. business
3. creative outlets
4. health
5. new ideas
6. sales & marketing
7. pleasures
8. needs
9. changes

10. moods
11. my website
12. promotions
13. family
14. finances
15. household projects
16. forgiveness
17. travel
18. next projects
19. friends
20. spirituality
21. sexuality
22. books
23. gratitude
24. marriage
25. children
26. writing
27. massage
28. frustrations
29. rituals
30. transitions
31. the future

If ever you get stuck, just note the date and refer to the number that corresponds with it on your list. For instance, if it is the 24th of the month, I may write about the current status of my marriage.

Note: Although I have seen different forms of this exercise in other journaling literature, I thank Kay Adams for first bringing "Topics Du Jour" to my attention in Journal to the Self (see bibliography).

Upon completion, reflect:

· How did this go for me?
· What did I learn?
· This brought up something new (what?)

(Record your mood after completing the exercise.)

Part One
Assignment #24

(Record your mood going into the exercise.)

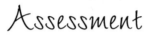

In the previous 23 assignments you have embarked on a journey of self-reflection that has taken you deeper into the self; both the light and shadow sides. Hopefully you have learned a little something about yourself along the way. Maybe you have even identified some patterns of behavior that no longer serve you, such as holding onto the past, self-sabotage, or giving away your power to others.

In today's exercise you are to write about what you've learned in this workshop. Notice which assignments were the most difficult. Ask yourself why. Have you altered your behavior in any way as a result of identifying what brings you joy?

Lastly, make a note of what you want to continue to explore in your journal. Go back and highlight the exercises you'd like to repeat.

I hope you have slowed down a bit, noticed more, and learned to be gently aware of what your needs are. I feel like I know you, like I'm sitting here reading over your shoulder as you bring this section of the workshop into completion. If you could see me, you would see that I am smiling and applauding your commitment to your personal growth. I wish you many blessings as you redefine who you are and become more of your authentic self.

Upon completion, reflect:

· How did this go for me?
· What did I learn?
· This brought up something new (what?)

(Record your mood after completing the exercise.)

Part One
Assignment #25

(Record your mood going into the exercise.)

Ending Up

I like rituals. I believe that there is something about the kinesthetic act that helps to imbed the meaning and the resulting therapeutic benefits of that process.

When I get to a point in my journal where I feel as if I am either stuck or tired, I ask myself, "Could this be complete?" Often the answer is a resounding yes. Even if I have only written half way through my journal I may decide that it is complete and time to move on.

At this time you need to make a decision as to what to do with your journal. Which brings us to today's exercise.

You may either keep your journal to look back and reflect upon or continue to use it independent of the workshop. Or you may decide to use the same journal as you move into Workshop Two.

If, on the other hand, you feel as if the work you have done here feels "heavy" and you would like to release your words, you may want to create a ritual of completion. Sometimes I actually burn my old journals as a way of releasing my attachment to the past and gaining a feeling of closure; especially if the journal was to work though a particularly difficult issue. Other times I tie up the journal with ribbon and put it away until I'm ready to decide.

Whatever you choose to do with your journal is a private matter. I do urge you, if you keep your journals, to give instructions to someone you trust as to where you keep them. Let that person know what you want done with them in the event of your death. This security measure may give you more freedom to write without censoring.

In any case, offer yourself a toast to the completion of this journal work. You deserve it.

When you're ready, move on to Workshop Two.

Upon completion, reflect:

· How did this go for me?
· What did I learn?
· This brought up something new (what?)

(Record your mood after completing the exercise.)

Journaling from the Heart

A Writing Workshop in Three Parts

Workshop Two

Paper Dreams:

Creating the Life you Crave

Introduction to Part Two

Now that you have redefined who you are, you are ready to define what you want. What is it that you crave? Where does your passion lie? What gives you the greatest pleasure?

I call the second part of this workshop "Paper Dreams" because by putting your yearnings on the page, you have taken the first step toward creating the life you desire.

We will address common issues such as fear of failure, perfectionism, and self-sabotage as well as how to recognize and defeat self-limiting thoughts and behaviors. By the end of this part of the workshop, you will hopefully be on your way to living the life you love and loving the life you live.

I have shared much of my own personal experience in this workshop because I think having done the work myself makes it more believable and easier for others to attempt.

Two of my favorite books on the topic of manifesting your dreams are *How Much Joy Can you Stand?*, by Suzanne Falter-Burns and *Write It Down, Make it Happen*, by Henriette Klauser. I cannot recommend these books highly enough for anyone who seeks to bring their dreams to life.
So let's dream big, shall we?

Part Two
Assignment #1

(Record your mood going into the exercise.)

Don't Look Now

Have you ever noticed how much easier it is to sing in the shower? Even if you know others are within earshot it doesn't seem to matter. Showers are like the "Free Space" on a Parcheesi board. Everyone is allowed to sing behind the curtain. The same thing happens in my ecstatic dance workshops. As soon as I turn down the lights and tell people to close their eyes, something happens. Inhibitions fall away and the wildness inside each one of the dancers is set free. Old people, fat people, awkward people, and people who don't believe they have a graceful bone in their bodies, suddenly become lost in the music.

Singer Susanna Clarke wrote, "You've Got to Dance like Nobody's Watching," and that lyric is a perfect quote for this exercise. Imagine that nobody's watching. Not a soul. Not your partner, your kids, your parents, and especially not the critics in your life; real or imagined.

What would you be doing? Not just here and now, but with your life? Write as if nobody's watching. Describe your life the way you'd like it to be. Do not limit yourself by lack of confidence, finances, or time.

Everyone has a dream, even you, whether you know it yet or not. You may feel that you have been so caught up in others' agendas that you've forgotten your dream, lost your passion. Fear not. The dream is still there, even if it lies dormant for now. We're going to try to wake it up.

Let your dream come to the surface and paint a new reality. Remember, nobody's watching.

Upon completion, reflect:

· How did this go for me?
· What did I learn?
· This brought up something new (what?)

(Record your mood after completing the exercise.)

Part Two
Assignment #2

(Record your mood going into the exercise.)

Making it Real

There is a picture postcard on my refrigerator of a beautiful yurt. A yurt is a round canvas and lattice frame shelter like those that Mongolian nomads build and tear down as they move from place to place. Today there are companies that make yurts that are sturdier and built for temporary or permanent lodging, depending upon how extravagant you want to get. In any case, I love the cozy way they look and I've always wanted to have one somewhere out in the boondocks. Someday I will.

I know this to be true, because whenever I begin with a thought and carry it into my physical environment, it soon becomes my reality. As far back as I can remember I have kept lists and pictures on my refrigerator and my bathroom mirror of the things I wanted to manifest in my life. Sooner or later the list gets shorter as I fill my life with what began as a mere image. Of course I continue to make new lists and add pictures.

Yesterday, or whenever it was that you completed Assignment One, you wrote out your dream. In today's exercise you are to find pictures that represent aspects of your dream. For instance, if your dream is to open a bookstore, you might select pictures of overstuffed chairs, shelves, or book covers. Make a list of the things your dream will require and tack it up where you can see it daily. Start a folder and collect articles, newspaper clippings or Internet printouts that relate to your dream.

Write in your journal about the things you have found. Write about how it feels to have tangible affirmations of your goals.

Upon completion, reflect:

· How did this go for me?
· What did I learn?
· This brought up something new (what?)

(Record your mood after completing the exercise.)

Part Two
Assignment # 3

(Record your mood going into the exercise.)

Excuses, Excuses

In Workshop One I explained how I personally sabotaged my walking program with a bunch of bogus excuses like, "It's too cold. I don't have a walking partner. I don't have time." Only when I was willing to be honest with myself, did I realize just how ridiculous my excuses were. At that point I was forced to choose what was most important: my health or my nice warm bed. It wasn't easy, but my health won out. A warm bed is no good if you can't get out of it without straining.

Whenever I start spewing a litany of excuses for not doing something, I remind myself to stop and consider my priorities. This is what I want you to do in today's exercise. Make a list of every excuse, every single thing that stands between you and your dream. Include both the valid and the bogus ones.

Then, sit down and cross off the list every excuse that you know is lame. You'll begin to recognize which ones are born out of your fear of success (which is a very real fear for many people) and which ones are those that you will have to work with in order to pursue your dream.

Once you have the list honed down, begin considering ways around these roadblocks. Get creative. Imagine that possibility exists in every thing.

It does.

Upon completion, reflect:

· How did this go for me?
· What did I learn?
· This brought up something new (what?)

(Record your mood after completing the exercise.)

Part Two
Assignment # 4

(Record your mood going into the exercise.)

What if?

Several years ago after tiring of real estate and knowing I had a new purpose brewing, I wondered to myself, "What if I became a massage therapist?" That thought was followed by, "What if I could get a scholarship to help with the tuition to the Healing Arts school?" The rest of the "what ifs" just seemed to tumble out, one after another.

"What if I could carpool with other students? What if the salon next to the real estate office would let me rent some space to do massage? What if I opened a practice while I was going to school so I would have clients to work with and some extra income?"

Within two months, all of the above came true. It wasn't magic or even sheer serendipity. The answers lay in determination, enthusiasm, and passion. I refused to believe there was anything to stop me from becoming a bodyworker.

So, what if you were to follow your dream? What would it take? Start by listing your "what ifs'" until you feel like you have outlined several possible options to get you from here to there. Let each question give birth to the next. Be prepared for an unexpected answer to your lingering doubts. Be prepared to live your dream.

(Recommended reading: "Whatif," a delightful poem by Shel Silverstein.)

Upon completion, reflect:

· How did this go for me?
· What did I learn?
· This brought up something new (what?)

(Record your mood after completing the exercise)

Part Two
Assignment # 5

(Record your mood going into the exercise.)

Steps

When my children were little and we lived in a two story house, it was always interesting to watch them learn to the climb stairs. What usually happened was that they would see something interesting going on up on the next level and their curiosity would be the catalyst for daring to venture upwards. On hands and knees they'd crawl, one step at a time, often pausing to look back down for a moment before continuing. Usually the desire to get to the top won out over their fears and they'd forge ahead, ever victorious to reach the summit (with Mommy biting her nails the whole way but cheering them on just the same).

Imagine that your dream is at the top of a stairway. All you need to do to reach it is to take one step at a time. You can even pause for a moment, consider how far you've come, and rejoice upon each tiny forward motion.

For today's exercise, you need to draw a set of steps. Label each step with one thing you need to do to bring you closer to your dream. For instance, remember that yurt I want to own? Well, I put on the bottom step, "order catalogs." That was easy enough. On the next step I wrote, "research yurts on the Internet for best quality/price." On the third step I wrote, "Open special savings account." The fourth step reads, "Cut out want ads for vacant property." "Research building codes" is on the fifth step. On the sixth step is "Run ad for possible co-housing opportunity." The seventh step reads "Call plumbers for quotes on running water." Next step, "Call electricians." The ninth step is to "beg, borrow or win the lottery." Until finally, I am at the top where I "order yurt."

This is obviously a simple representation as there will be much more involved, but it helps to keep focused on just one step at a time. Buy some stickers or gold stars to place on your stairs each time you move up a step. Don't forget the reward waiting at the top.

Write in your journal about your steps. What have you done today to bring you closer to your dream?

Upon completion, reflect:

· How did this go for me?
· What did I learn?
· This brought up something new (what?)

(Record your mood after completing the exercise.)

Part Two
Assignment # 6

(Record your mood going into the exercise.)

Fear of Failure

In one of my other lives, I imagined myself running a cozy little daycare center in my home. I was pregnant with my son at the time and I thought it would be a great way to make enough money to stay home with him.

I hired a contractor to finish our attic into the perfect space for a daycare. I took a course on childcare and became licensed in my city. I shopped garage sales and filled the room with toys, books, and a little table and chairs. The room turned out wonderfully and I ran an ad in the paper to solicit a little tribe of children to fill my space.

I was about seven months pregnant when I opened my business with four children. Within three weeks I knew that I had made a horrible mistake. I was exhausted. I lost patience with parents who showed up late or not at all. I was irritable. I sat in my lovely upstairs room and cried. I was embarrassed to admit to these parents, my husband, and myself, that I had really goofed. I was not cut out to be somebody else's mother and I was certainly not a stay-home mom.

Failure? Not really. I learned a valuable lesson. Fortunately I had not given up my real estate license so I still had a job and found that I could take my baby with me to work much of the time. The bonus was that my son got all those toys and books and a beautiful playroom!

Write about your fears. What is the worst thing that could happen if you were to take the risk of pursuing your dream? Write about past "failures" and what valuable lessons you have learned from them.

Upon completion, reflect:

· How did this go for me?
· What did I learn?
· This brought up something new (what?)

(Record your mood after completing the exercise.)

Part Two
Assignment # 7

(Record your mood going into the exercise.)

Money

Most dreams (not all) require money. For some, money is not an issue. Perhaps you are blessed with a reservoir of funds to help fuel your dream. But for many of you, money may be a real issue in pursuing your dream.

If you are not financially secure, you have two choices: 1. Find a dream that's cheap, or, 2. Find a way to finance your dream.

The first choice will make your dream easier to achieve (financially). For example, if your goal is to lose weight and establish a healthy lifestyle, you may not have to spend an extra dime. You can choose to walk rather than join the gym and buying less junk food will actually save you money.

But if your dream is to open a coffee shop, then that's a different story. For continuity's sake, I'll use my yurt as an example. I don't happen to have an extra $15,000 lying around. However I do have equity in my home and I could borrow against that. But what of those who don't have this option or don't want to go into debt? Get creative!

My plan is to contact a lot of yurt companies and offer to provide access to my yurt as a "model home" in exchange for a significant discount off the price of the materials. I also plan to barter with folks to help with set-up and any plumbing or electrical work I need done. And I'm going to try to find a landowner who will allow me to put up my yurt on his or her property at a minimal fee rather than buying land.

Your assignment today is to brainstorm ways to bring you closer to your dream. If yours is not one that costs money, brainstorm ways to find an abundance of support in the emotional sense. Do not edit out the things that sound ridiculous. You never know what might work. There are people with money looking for ways to invest it. There are programs for new entrepreneurs. There are grants, fellowships and scholarships waiting to be filled. Let yourself dream in a big way.

Upon completion, reflect:

· How did this go for me?
· What did I learn?
· This brought up something new (what?)

(Record your mood after completing the exercise.)

Part Two
Assignment # 8

(Record your mood going into the exercise.)

Rain on the Parade

I once had this great idea (I thought it was great) to gather a bunch of my friends together and go out to eat at an Indian restaurant. Have you ever watched Indian people dine? They eat with their hands. They use flat bread to scoop their food and they do it without making a mess. It is not as easy as it looks. One of my clients happens to own an Indian restaurant with his wife. When I asked him about it, he offered to have his wife demonstrate for our party how to eat in the traditional Indian way.

I was so excited I told one of my best friends. He said, "Why would anyone want to eat with their hands if they could use utensils?"

I was devastated. I thought everyone would think my idea was fun and adventurous. So I thought for a moment and then I said, "Why would anyone want to finger paint if they could use a brush?"

Do you know what he said? He said, "My point exactly." I swear to you that's what he said. It was then that I realized he was raining on my proverbial parade. He was being what Julia Cameron, the guru of The Artist's Way, would call a Wet Blanket. These folks are bad news around Idea People and Artists. So I decided not to listen to my friend. I told several other friends and you know what? All of them thought it was a wonderful idea.

In today's exercise, you are to make two columns in your journal and label them "People Who Support My Dream" and "Rain Clouds." The latter, of course, are people who do not support your dream.

When you are finished look at your list. Surround yourself as often as possible with the people in the first column. Find more people to add to that list. Avoid the people on the second list, or at the very least, don't tell them about your dream and its progress. They don't get to share in your dream.

Upon completion, reflect:

· How did this go for me?
· What did I learn?
· This brought up something new (what?)

(Record your mood after completing the exercise.)

Part Two
Assignment # 9

(Record your mood going into the exercise.)

Simply Divine

There was a time when I thought I could not have my dreams because there simply wasn't enough time, energy and resources to go around. There was so much to do, so many people-things-animals-plants to take care of, and my to-do list was endless.

I can't pinpoint exactly when it happened, but I think I was watching a rerun of Seinfeld, when the thought occurred to me that if I turned off the television, I could get several things done that I hadn't been able to get to earlier in the day. Now, I really liked Seinfeld and even enjoyed the reruns, (although I always hated the commercials and muted them) so giving up that half-hour seemed like a big thing... until I did it. It felt so good to be caught up that I decided to skip TV the next night to do something else: read. I hadn't had time to read in so long, a stack of books had piled up on my nightstand.

In case you haven't already guessed, I lost interest in TV as I realized I was suddenly gifted with an abundance of time. The following week I pulled the plug completely (with my husband's agreement and much whining from my son) on television. My son soon forgot and went back to reading! My husband and I wondered aloud how we had ever found the time to watch TV in the first place.

My point is that there are lots of ways to simplify your life and have more time and energy if you look closely. Kill your TV. Skip the newspaper. Get rid of high-maintenance items. Give up some of your committees. Spend less time on the phone/computer.

In today's exercise, make a list of things you can do to simplify your life.

From this day forward ask yourself daily, "What one thing did I do today to bring me closer to my dream?" Write your answer in your journal (every day) as a reminder that you are committed to a fulfilling life.

Upon completion, reflect:

· How did this go for me?
· What did I learn?
· This brought up something new (what?)

(Record your mood after completing the exercise.)

Part Two
Assignment # 10

(Record your mood going into the exercise.)

Champions

The first time I heard the song, "You are the Wind Beneath my Wings," I cried. I was at a wedding reception and they played it during the father-daughter dance. It was obvious from watching the bride look into her dad's eyes that he really was her hero.

I think we all need role models to look up to. Especially when we're working hard to pursue a dream. There may be people out there who have accomplished something similar to what you want, who can hold up a beacon of light to lead the way.

There is a woman who lives nearby me who has written a book every year for the last several years. She lives with her mother and has a simple life. Her writing is divine. Over the past few years, each of her books has fared a little better than the last. Recently, she published a novel that Kirkus Reviews called "A Masterpiece." Movie rights were sold. She is suddenly famous and financially more secure than most writers dream about. But from what I know of this woman, she will probably stay where she is and continue writing a novel each year because this is what she loves. She is one who holds a light for me.

Think about your role models. What men and women have gone before you and shown you that there is a way? Write about them. Write *to* them if they're still living. Imagine what it was they had or did that made them a success at accomplishing a dream. Imagine yourself following the map they have kindly laid out for you.

Upon completion, reflect:

· How did this go for me?
· What did I learn?
· This brought up something new (what?)

(Record your mood after completing the exercise.)

Part Two
Assignment #11

(Record your mood going into the exercise.)

I Think I Can

When I wrote my first book, it became obvious that I would need to build a presence on the web in order to successfully get the word out about my product. That meant building a web page.

Now, I'm the sort of person who depends on her right brain to do most of the work, but I'm also just stubborn (and frugal) enough to try almost anything. So off I went to carve out my little corner in cyberspace.

For those of you that have never dealt with html (the language used to write web pages) it is pretty intimidating, especially to non-detail people like me. I took one look and threw up my arms. Enter Wayne, my faithful tutor and patience-facilitator. He sat beside me as we took baby-steps through learning just enough html to update my page from time to time. Over a period of a couple of months, I was not only updating my pages; I was creating new ones by the dozen. Wayne now refers to me as one of his best "I can't" converts.

So often we limit ourselves by beliefs that are set up to save us from failure. Unfortunately, these self-limiting beliefs serve only to keep us from swelling into our fullest potential.

Today, make a list of self-limiting beliefs, such as "I'm not out-going enough," or "I can't learn that," etc., etc. When you've written as many as you can think of, re-write these beliefs in the opposite, limitless voice. For example, "I can be outgoing when I'm excited about something" or "I am open to learning new things."

Upon completion, reflect:

· How did this go for me?
· What did I learn?
· This brought up something new (what?)

(Record your mood after completing the exercise)

Part Two
Assignment # 12

(Record your mood going into the exercise.)

I Told You So

I remember very clearly the day I wrote my first book, *Loose Ends*, in my head. I came home from a beautiful walk and quickly began jotting down all my ideas. Then, I typed up a "pretend" book and started showing it around to friends. Each person I handed it to I told, "This is the book I'm writing." And each time I said that, my stomach did a little flip. Who did I think I was, telling people that I was going to write and publish a book?

But you know, every time I said those words, it got a little easier and I believed it a little more. By the time I had told about a dozen people, I not only sounded confident, I had convinced myself that I was about to be an author and I was going to learn the publishing business. Basically, I said I was, therefore I was!

Sound easy? It is. You just start acting as if you are doing what it is you want to do (or being what it is you want to be.) If your dream is to lose thirty pounds, start carrying yourself as if you feel thirty pounds lighter. If your dream is to be a writer, tell people you are a writer (and for crying out loud, write!) And if your dream is teach, well then I suggest you get some cards printed up and start "being" a teacher. If you believe it, others will too.

Today's assignment is in two parts. The first part is to write in your journal AS IF you are already living your dream. Write in the present tense. Write about how it feels. Write so that you can taste your dream and others will taste it too. Record a day in your new life.

The second part is to tell at least one new person each day what you are doing. You will not jinx yourself. On the contrary, you will become what you say you are. Trust me. Your subconscious believes every word you say. You may as well tell it what you want it to hear.

If you live your dream, you will give your dream life!

Upon completion, reflect:

· How did this go for me?
· What did I learn?
· This brought up something new (what?)

(Record your mood after completing the exercise.)

Part Two
Assignment # 13

(Record your mood going into the exercise.)

Bill of Rights

When I began home schooling my son, I found that one of the most challenging aspects was not preparing assignments or checking work, but maintaining a level of respect from him as his teacher, while also filling the role of his mother. The line between these two roles often became blurred, causing wrinkles in our relationship. I wanted him to offer me the same respect he would his teacher, or more so, since he loves me. But it was difficult for him to adjust to my new role.

Today's exercise comes as a result of how I handled this problem with my son. We each wrote out our own "Bill of Rights;" mine as teacher and his as student to clarify our needs and demand observance of our rights. Part of what Jacob wrote is this:

- I have a right to return to public school next year if I choose to.
- I have a right to the same holiday and semester breaks as public school kids get.
- I have a right to ask for help if I don't understand an assignment.

My Bill of Rights included:

- I have a right to expect you to finish work I assign you.
- I have a right not to be argued with or badgered.
- I have a right to do my own work without being interrupted just because you are home.

We signed each other's statement and agreed to do our best to keep each other's rights in mind as we operated our little home school. The exercise was so successful, we ended up writing a separate set of "Personal" rights.

Today, write a "Bill of Rights" for yourself. I suggest framing it and putting it up where others can see it, as well as to refer to yourself. You might include such rights as privacy, the freedom to pursue your dream, rewards, time alone, or whatever it is that you may need reminding that you deserve.

Upon completion, reflect:

˙ How did this go for me?
˙ What did I learn?
˙ This brought up something new (what?)

(Record your mood after completing the exercise.)

Part Two
Assignment #14

(Record your mood going into the exercise.)

Oh Baby

When I was pregnant with my first child, I was only eighteen; nearly a child yet myself. What did I know about raising a baby? How on earth was I going to know what to do with this new life? "Wait!" I pleaded. "I can't do this."

Of course, I did do it and although I'm certain I made a lot of mistakes along the way, my daughter grew up to be healthy, happy, and a wonderful human being who is now a mother herself.

Your dream is a lot like a pregnancy, especially now in this, the gestation period. Think of that first idea you had as an egg. Think of the passion and excitement surrounding your idea as that which fertilized your egg. Suddenly you were pregnant with a dream, just waiting to be born.

In the first trimester, many mothers get nauseous. Did you feel a few waves of queasiness when you realized that you had stepped over the line between having a thought (your dream) and giving that thought form? The fears, the worries, the insecurities; these are all typical symptoms of early pregnancy... and making life transitions.

But by now, you are most likely into the second trimester of gestating your dream. Picture your dream as a fire in your belly, and each step you take that brings you closer together as the blood pumping through an invisible umbilical cord. Feed your dream with visualization, affirmations, and a positive attitude. Breathe deeply. Get lots of exercise and take naps when you're tired. Put your feet up.

Write about how it feels to be carrying this dream inside of you. Write about your excitement. Write about your fears. Write about expectations. Go out and buy your "baby" a gift; something to nurture your dream such as a how-to book or an accessory.

For instance I'm going to buy a welcome mat for the front door of my yurt and a hanging for the walls. Act as if you are expecting your dream!

Upon completion, reflect:

· How did this go for me?
· What did I learn?
· This brought up something new (what?)

(Record your mood after completing the exercise.)

Part Two
Assignment #15

(Record your mood going into the exercise.)

Choices

In the old paradigm (the way we were before we became accountable for our own happiness) we were told that whatever happened was left in the hands of the gods or Lady Luck or a roll of the cosmic dice. When we no longer accepted that idea, we sometimes blamed others for our misery, even God, because that was still easier than taking responsibility for our own lives. Unfortunately, many of us then stepped into the "should" role. We convinced ourselves that if we did the right thing, our lives would turn out the way we wanted them to. Unfortunately, that only left us shouldering guilt, regret, and impossible expectations.

Finally, we arrived here, in this present place where we make conscious choices in an effort to live our lives more mindfully and with an open heart; one that is entitled to passion and bliss.

Today's exercise comes to you in five parts.

1. Write down a list of ten things you once believed were purely fate or luck (good or bad).

2. Write down who you felt at the time was responsible for each of those events.

3. Write down anything that you may have felt you "should" have done differently to affect the outcome of these ten things.

4. Write a new list of ten things, ten conscious choices you are making now, to create the life you want

5. Write yourself a letter of pardon, forgiving yourself (and others, if you wish) for every time you felt you screwed up, took a wrong turn, or failed to act appropriately in a given situation. That was then and this is now. Let it go.

Upon completion, reflect:

· How did this go for me?
· What did I learn?
· This brought up something new (what?)

(Record your mood after completing the exercise.)

Part Two
Assignment #16

(Record your mood going into the exercise.)

Unfinished Business

For years I had a pile of books by my nightstand and several more in the bookcase that were tagged with a bookmark to identify how far I had read, or seen in another light, how much further I had to go before I could breathe a sigh of relief upon completion. Every time I passed a book with a marker sticking out of the top, I'd get a little twitch in my gut. *You need to finish those*, a little voice inside me would say.

It wasn't just books that went unfinished. There was an afghan I'd started when I was pregnant that became low on the priority list once the baby arrived (ten years ago!) There was the book I'd started writing about watching my mother die. There were unfinished art projects, partially completed scrapbooks, and a plethora of other incomplete pieces of good intentions surrounding me. And they were all screaming "Finish me!" from every corner of the house. Guilt-ridden, I refused to allow myself to begin any fresh projects until I completed the ones I'd started.

Then one day I had an epiphany of sorts. I realized that I was not only using the incomplete projects as an excuse for not doing what I passionately wanted to do, I was actually sabotaging my best intentions by allowing these dangling details to get in the way of my dreams.

Here's what I did. I went around and closed every open book that I had no burning desire to finish. I plucked out a fistful of bookmarkers. I dumped all my unfinished projects inside a box and took it to the Goodwill, forcing myself to remain detached from what I knew I would never finish. Then I stood in the middle of the living room and I said, "Done!"

I cannot begin to describe the euphoria that spread through my body and soul. I felt a release so boundless I swear I must have lost ten pounds of guilt.

Now it's your turn. Give yourself permission to close the book on those things you no longer need to finish. Un-should yourself. Get rid of what tugs at your guilt-strings. Have a celebration. Then write about your experience.

Upon completion, reflect:

· How did this go for me?
· What did I learn?
· This brought up something new (what?)

(Record your mood after completing the exercise.)

Part Two
Assignment #17

(Record your mood going into the exercise.)

Best Wishes

When I was a little girl I wished for roller skates with pink puff balls on the toes, just like Susie Buttleman's. Susie even had a matching pink case for her skates. Whenever our elementary school had a roller skating party, I would watch with envy as Susie laced up those beautiful white skates and coasted off with all the boys' palms sweating at the thought of holding Susie's hand during the "couples skate."

I didn't get those skates, and I think I know why. One, because our family of nine was too poor to afford new roller skates, and secondly, because I didn't ask. I didn't ask because I didn't really believe I would get them. But now as I think back, I wonder if I had asked, if I had wished hard enough, would it have been me skating hand in hand with Mark Andersen over to the counter for a blue moon ice cream cone?

Maybe not. But maybe. Since that time I have come to realize that I do often get what I wish for. Especially if I ask for it. Sometimes just because I wish so hard I begin to believe I will get what I long for. Like moving to California. I wished and I asked and I wished some more and by gosh here I am in paradise.

Your job today is to remember the innocence of your childhood. Find a star, if you like, or a fountain, and wish away. Bake a cake and light a candle on top for every wish you can think of before you blow out the flames. Believe in the magic and the power of wishes. But be careful what you wish for, because dreams really do come true! Write your wishes.

Upon completion, reflect:

- How did this go for me?
- What did I learn?
- This brought up something new (what?)

(Record your mood after completing the exercise.)

Part Two
Assignment #18

(Record your mood going into the exercise.)

Helping Hands

When I finished writing my book, *Loose Ends*, I knew I would need to learn page layout in order to ready my manuscript for the printer. In the old days you could just type your pages, print them out, and send them in as "boards" to be filmed during the pre-press operation. Now almost every print job is taken from a disk and printed according to how the pages are laid out in a specific software program.

Enter PageMaker. If you've never worked with this program, then I probably can only tell you that learning how to use this software is somewhere up there with learning to speak Russian. Backwards. I spent a lot of money on the program itself. I spent even more on a couple of books that were supposed to teach me how to implement this wonderful program. I was determined to teach myself.

Thirty-some hair-pulling hours later, I threw up my hands in agony. I described to one of my clients what an awful time I was having. She asked, "Why don't you have someone help you?" I answered that I was trying to save money. She replied,

"So how many hours have you spent trying to learn it and how much is your time worth?" She had a point.

I did find someone to help me and I even bartered with her for massage to placate my frugal self. What's more, when I ran out of time, I hired someone to layout the next book. Why? Because, as the Loreal commercial goes, "I'm worth it."

And so are you. Is it difficult for you to delegate? Do you recognize the value of your time? If you allowed someone else to do part of the work, just think how much closer to your dream you could be.

Write down the things with which you could use some help. Make a list of all the people who might be able to help you do some of the things on your list. Then, contact them and ask. The worst thing that could happen is that they could say no. Are you hesitant about asking for help? Write about that too.

Upon completion, reflect:

· How did this go for me?
· What did I learn?
· This brought up something new (what?)

(Record your mood after completing the exercise.)

Part Two
Assignment #19

(Record your mood going into the exercise.)

Check Up

Just like you, I get excited about my dreams. I really want that yurt and I want to finish my novel this year. I've been riding along with you as I write these assignments, feeling my passion fueled by the writing and the commitment to actively pursuing my dreams. Yet, every once in a while I pause to reflect upon just exactly how far I've come.

I have a picture of that yurt right here by my desk. I've called someone who owns a yurt and made an appointment to go see what living in one is like. I've even cut out an ad for a used yurt. And I finally got up the nerve to tell my husband what I'm up to. (He wasn't thrilled about the yurt, but I think he finds my enthusiasm endearing.)

Today is a good day for you to reflect. What one thing did you do today to bring you closer to your dream? With whom have you shared your dream? What new pictures have you added to your dream file? What phone calls have you made? What classes have you enrolled in?

Write about every little thing you can think of that you have done since you began this workshop that demonstrates your choice to give life to your dream. Remind yourself how important this dream is.

When you are finished, applaud yourself for being brave and open and alive with imagination. Remember your purpose. Keep the dream alive.

Upon completion, reflect:

· How did this go for me?
· What did I learn?
· This brought up something new (what?)

(Record your mood after completing the exercise.)

(Record your mood going into the exercise.)

The Last Trimester

If I can borrow once again from the analogy of pregnancy we used in Assignment # 14, (sorry guys!) it's time to prepare for the birth of your dream. As you bring your dream to life, remember that sometimes there are labor pains and sometimes they are agonizing, but just keep breathing (Don't say that to a pregnant women in transitional labor, however. Especially if her teeth are close to your body.)

I imagine if you are like me that you are swelling with anticipation. You know the time is near and that it is up to you to be ready for the Big Event. However, unlike childbirth, your dream may be a slow unfolding. Or not. Maybe your dream hinges on one Big Thing and as soon as that Thing happens, viola! Your dream is hatched.

Think of this as that period just before birth. Often there is a calm. Sometimes there is a great urge to clean corners as we make room for this wonderful new extension of ourselves. My example:

Well, here we are, waiting. I have been planning for this since the day I was born. Each chapter has been lovingly and tenderly formed until now, when all that is left is a little editing here and a little polishing there. I am so excited! I am so hopeful...

Are you ready to live your dream? Write about the impending birth of your dream. Write about it as if you have been planning your whole life around this moment.

Upon completion, reflect:

· How did this go for me?
· What did I learn?
· This brought up something new (what?)

(Record your mood after completing the exercise.)

Part Two
Assignment #21

(Record your mood going into the exercise.)

Just Rewards

I got up at four o'clock this morning to finish the editing on Workshops One and Three of this book. I don't usually do things in order, and this book is no exception. I have to admit that I think I was saving Workshop Two for last because it is my favorite. I truly enjoy being a part of other people's journey toward living the life they dream.

It is now nearly seven in the evening, and I have only stopped twice to grab a quick bite. For nearly fifteen hours I've been sitting here plugging away at this book. As you may imagine, I love what I do. But I'm beginning to lose the feeling in my feet as my circulation suffers from being in this position for too many hours. My neck is tired and my back is sore. I'm not whining, I'm noticing what my body is trying to tell me.

Tomorrow I plan to get a massage. Not just because I need it, but because I think it is important to reward oneself for hard work and perseverance. In fact, I'm going to splurge and get an extra half-hour plus a facial. Oh what the heck, I think I'll sign up for a pedicure too.

Today's exercise, as you may have guessed, is to reward yourself in some way for doing whatever it has taken to bring you this far. Even if you don't feel like you've done "enough," it is important to acknowledge that you are enough and you deserve a reward.

Write about how it feels to accomplish what you have done so far. Write about how you want to reward yourself. Then do it. And when you have your reward, write about how it felt to gift yourself with pleasure.

Upon completion, reflect:

· How did this go for me?
· What did I learn?
· This brought up something new (what?)

(Record your mood after completing the exercise.)

Part Two
Assignment #22

(Record your mood going into the exercise.)

Why?

Sometimes I ask myself why I work so hard, spend so much time giving of my time and energy to help others. Between home schooling my son, maintaining a therapeutic massage practice, writing books and articles, and facilitating workshops, I spend a lot of time in service to others.

Obviously, I do what I do because it is a passion of mine. I learned a long time ago that I only have myself to blame if I'm not doing what I love. However, when you are working hard to further your dream(s), you may need reminding just what it is that makes it all worthwhile.

In the previous exercise, you rewarded yourself for working hard at giving life to your dream. Today, we reflect on the naturally occurring rewards that come as a result of living our dream. The purpose is to remind yourself why it is you dreamed this in the first place.

Here is a sampling from my list for my yurt dream:

1. I'll get to spend time in nature
2. It will be peaceful
3. No phones means no interruptions
4. The windows will offer me much-needed sunlight while I'm working or relaxing
5. I can dance my heart out
6. I get to shower outdoors
7. I will enjoy a sense of accomplishment
8. I will own my own private writing retreat
9. I will be living lightly on the earth

Keep your list going for as long as you can, and add to it as you think of more rewards. You should easily be able to come up with twenty-five rewards for achieving your dream.

Upon completion, reflect:

· How did this go for me?
· What did I learn?
· This brought up something new (what?)

(Record your mood after completing the exercise.)

Part Two
Assignment #23

(Record your mood going into the exercise.)

The Wise Self Visits Again

In Workshop One (if you completed it) you received a visit from your ninety year-old self. The purpose of that visit was to connect to your inner wisdom. Today we are going to go back out on the porch for another appointment. This time, we're going to look back on your life as it might be.

Most seniors, if you ask them, will tell you it is not what they did in their life that they regret, but what they didn't do. The roads not taken. The opportunities turned down.

In this exercise, write from your Wise Self's point of view. Let your Wisdom speak to you about what might be if your dream becomes a reality. Ask your Wise Self about those fears you have and what might happen. Have a conversation about how it was, living this dream.

As you write, ask any questions that might come up and wait for an answer. Let your Wise Self reassure you. Let him or her give you advice. Do your best to imagine that this is you, only wiser. You already know what is important in the Big Picture.

Oh, and don't forget the glass of lemonade.

Upon completion, reflect:

· How did this go for me?
· What did I learn?
· This brought up something new (what?)

(Record your mood after completing the exercise.)

Part Two
Assignment #24

(Record your mood going into the exercise.)

The Big Event

It's here! Today we're going to write about the birth of your dream.

What a joy and a privilege it has been to sit here writing these words to you. I feel the bliss a midwife must feel as she tends to her expectant parents. If you could see me, you would see that I am smiling proudly. If you could hear me, you would hear much cheering and clapping.

Even if you have not "materialized' your dream yet, if you have followed this workshop with a mindful intent, you will be experiencing changes in your life that will continue to bring you closer to living a more passionate life.

In today's exercise, write about this moment. Have you accomplished what you hoped to in this workshop? More? If not, why not? What have you learned about your dream? How does it feel to be steering your own ship? What new friendships have you been afforded as a result of seeking support? What relationships have you outgrown? Most importantly, are you ready to live your dreams?

Afterwards, go back and as you did at the end of Workshop One, write about the exercises that were the most difficult for you. What was it that made these assignments challenging? Highlight those you may want to repeat at a future time.

Upon completion, reflect:

· How did this go for me?
· What did I learn?
· This brought up something new (what?)

(Record your mood after completing the exercise.)

Part Two
Assignment #25

(Record your mood going into the exercise.)

It's a...!

Here you are. It's time to announce to the world (or just to yourself) the birth of your "baby." In this assignment, fill out the following information in your Workshop Journal. Make a copy. Frame it. Hang it. Live it.

_____is proud to announce the
birth of _____
on this _____ day of _____
2,0_____.

The proud parent is doing well and looks forward to a wonderful relationship with this new part of his/her life.

You can change the wording to suit your "dream." For example I could fill in the weight and height of my yurt or my finished novel. Send copies of your annoucement out to your friends and family.

Just for fun, add your own handprints for effect. When was the last time you finger painted?

Congratulations. You've done well. Have a (bubblegum) cigar.

Upon completion, reflect:

· How did this go for me?
· What did I learn?
· This brought up something new (what?)

(Record your mood after completing the exercise.)

Journaling from the Heart

A Writing Workshop in Three Parts

Workshop Three

Waking the Muse:
Toward More Creative Journaling

Introduction to Part Three

The final leg of the workshop takes you to the next level of journal writing: Creative Journaling. It has been my experience that over time, many of you will begin to notice poetic phrases, interesting stories, and intriguing characters sprinkled throughout your journals. You may find yourself no longer writing for the therapeutic benefit of self-discovery alone, but for the simple pleasure in the act of writing. Perhaps you even yearn to become published.

The following exercises are offered as more creative techniques for reflection, description, dialogue, and story telling. You may even end up with a few gems worth polishing up for submission. The goal of this workshop, however, is not necessarily to write for publication but for the pure joy of it.

The most important thing to remember is to let yourself (and your words) be free. Consider every writing a rough draft. There is no need to make corrections as you write. In fact, doing so will hamper your creativity and make your Muse crabby. It is better just to keep your pen to the page (or your fingers to the keyboard) and write.

You will continue to learn about yourself through these exercises. Hopefully, you will also find much reward in the writing itself.

Part Three
Assignment # 1

(Record your mood going into the exercise.)

Who is this Writer?

It is difficult to be objective when writing about yourself. We cloud our descriptions with judgement and self-doubt. Have you ever been introduced by someone who described you in a way you didn't realize you are perceived? Perhaps this is because they are on the outside looking in.

Just for today, go outside of yourself and peer in. Introduce yourself from the third person point of view. Use she/he instead of I. Tell how you got from "there" to "here." Tell what you notice about yourself as you write this.

For example, I might write:

Eldonna is wondering if you will understand what she wants you to accomplish in this exercise. As she writes, she tilts just a bit to the left, as she has always done. Perhaps this is because she is trying so hard to access that side of her brain in order to bring balance to her writing.

Write as if you are describing yourself to a friend. You are.

Introducing... you!

Upon completion, reflect:

· How did this go for me?
· What did I learn?
· This brought up something new (what?)

(Record your mood after completing the exercise.)

Part Three
Assignment #2

(Record your mood going into the exercise)

Journal Letter

How often have you wished you could just come out and ask your journal to give you the answers to your questions without having to go through all the work of writing, writing, writing until you finally figure out what you already knew in your gut anyway?

That's exactly what you're going to do today. You're going to ask your journal for answers and you're going to tell your journal what you need from it. You're going to be honest. Don't edit yourself. Just start writing. Here is an example (but try not to let it influence your entry).

Dear Journal:

I know that I have it in me to write great stuff but when I come to the blank page I just freeze up. My writing falls flat. I lose access to all those great ideas I had when I was driving on the highway.

How can I tap into my creativity? Will you help me find my writing voice? Will you help me create believable dialogue? Will you help me find ways to describe settings and create exciting climaxes and intriguing plots? Will you help me to establish rhythm in my poetry?

I need you to record all my ideas, all my mistakes, every epiphany as I discover the Creator within. Thank you for not judging or criticizing me. Thank you for providing a safe place to write freely.

Hopefully Yours,

A. Budding Writer

Okay now it's your turn. Write a letter to your journal asking for what you need with regard to your writing. Be specific. Direct questions are the most apt to receive direct answers.

Upon completion, reflect:

· How did this go for me?
· What did I learn?
· This brought up something new (what?)

(Record your mood after completing the exercise.)

Part Three
Assignment #3

(Record your mood going into the exercise.)

Behind You

You are who you are because of every experience you have had, every person you've loved and been loved by, and all the tiny pieces of life that make up your history. Often, we get caught up in the trail behind us rather than the path that is laid out in front of our feet. Sometimes all that is needed is to record what is behind us in order to move forward.

In this exercise you will simply write, "I come from..." and just let whatever flows follow. Write for as long as it takes to get you from there to here. It doesn't necessarily have to be a record of events. It can be a record of your emotional or spiritual history.

Example:

I come from simple. Simple times, simple people, simple life. But simple didn't always mean easy.

Write about where/what you come from. Bring yourself from there to here so that you can be fully present in your continued writing. You may find memories triggered that you had forgotten. Jot them down as separate writing exercises.

Upon completion, reflect:

· How did this go for me?
· What did I learn?
· This brought up something new (what?)

(Record your mood after completing the exercise.)

Part Three
Assignment #4

(Record your mood going into the exercise)

Upside Down

You can tell a lot about a person by what they carry with them: in their car, in their purse/briefcase or in their pockets. Not the ordinary stuff like barrettes and matches, but the things that reveal the inner person.

I once had an interviewee empty his pockets on the table in front of us. He pulled out a jade stone, four divining rods, and a set of keys to a 1971 Westphalia. It was one of the best stories I have ever gotten.

If I were to turn you upside down, what would fall out that would tell the story of you? What would I learn that I would never think to ask you about? What is the most peculiar of these items?

Describe at least three things that would pique the interest of a stranger (or even someone who thinks they know you) from the contents of your person. Ignore the boring stuff and go right to the goodies. What secrets do your pockets hold?

Hint: If you are someone who carries nothing more than the bare necessities with you, what does the lack of "things" say about you? On the other hand, if your purse and your car are filled to the brim with "just in case" items, what do we already know about you?

Upon completion, reflect:

· How did this go for me?
· What did I learn?
· This brought up something new (what?)

(Record your mood after completing the exercise.)

Part Three
Assignment #5

(Record your mood going into the exercise)

A Fly on the Wall

Most of us come into contact with lots of other people on a daily basis. You may actually interact with only one or two others on a given day or you may have an exchange (including a smile or a wave) with hundreds of people. There are also people on the periphery of your days; the ones you don't interact with but who linger on the edges of your everyday life. These are the ones I want you to pay the most attention to today.

Be a fly on the wall at your place of employment, in a café, or in the park. Look around and notice who is part of your world. Choose one or two "characters" and write about them. Describe this person in great detail using all of your senses, even if you're not close enough to know for sure. Make up the details you cannot know. Do your best to stay out of judgement of the person in order that you write more freely. Tell this person's story. Where did she come from? What is his job, if he has one? Write specifically. For example:

Lyle stands in front of the café trying to look casual but the twitch in his jaw gives him away. He's waiting for her, another blind date that his stupid roommate has set him up with again. His wrinkled khaki pants give away his bachelorhood. He sniffs his armpit, as if no one will see the relief in his face when all he smells is antiperspirant.

Do you see how easy it is to make up another's reality? Even as I began writing about this man I already had decided what his date would look like, how it would end, and what he would be thinking as he fell asleep.

Take off the screens that keep you from seeing past your immediate environment. Tell a story.

Upon completion, reflect:

· How did this go for me?
· What did I learn?
· This brought up something new (what?)

(Record your mood after completing the exercise.)

Part Three
Assignment #6

(Record your mood going into the exercise)

Conversations

Many writers often have audible exchanges with themselves. Thinking out loud is a way of structuring your thoughts and laying down the beginnings of an oral history. When we tell stories to our children and to our children's children, it is a way to imbed those stories so that they may be told and retold again and again.

Talking to oneself might be perceived as a bit eccentric, however, by talking to yourself in your journal you not only practice your oral history or story outline, you get a chance to find out what response your words might induce. Here is a practice dialogue:

"I know I just had those keys in my hand. Where the heck could they have gone?"

"Try looking by the phone."

"I already looked there. Why do I lose so many things!"

"You're trying to do too much, that's why. Slow down, for crying out loud."

"Slow down? Slow down! How in the hell am I supposed to
slow down? I don't get everything done as it is."

"That's because you're always rushing. You have to go back and
redo things because you messed up by hurrying through it."

"I know that, but I'm so stressed."

"You need a break. Why don't you go bum around downtown
for a while. Have a cup of coffee or visit the art museum."

"Yeah. That's what I need to do.."

In this journal dialogue the writer is holding down both sides
of the conversation. He is answering his own questions because the dialogue is a way to access those answers that reside
within.

Have a dialogue with yourself in your journal. Present a current problem or question and then let the conversation unfold.
Be alert to the hidden messages as well as the obvious ones.

Upon completion, reflect:

· How did this go for me?
· What did I learn?
· This brought up something new (what?)

(Record your mood after completing the exercise.)

Part Three
Assignment #7

(Record your mood going into the exercise)

Musical Pens

Music can sometimes be a distraction when writing but there are times when it can also inspire. Personally I tend to want to get up and dance if there is music playing. However this exercise uses the music to help you explore the possibilities of your imagination.

In today's assignment, you will choose a piece of music from one of the following classifications and write about where it takes you. Or you can choose more than one to compare the experiences. Select cuts that have no lyrics.

1. New Age
2. Classical
3. World Music (African, S. American, Indian, etc.)

Play the music with your eyes closed. Wait until it is finished before you write. Did you see pictures? What feeling did the music invoke? Where did it take you? Write about what you "saw" in between the notes.

Tell a story against the backdrop of your music.

Upon completion, reflect:

· How did this go for me?
· What did I learn?
· This brought up something new (what?)

(Record your mood after completing the exercise.)

Part Three
Assignment #8

(Record your mood going into the exercise.)

Behind the Door

We are offered many paths in our lives and in our writing. The thing that makes every life and every story unique is that not only are each of us very different, but we make different choices based upon our own personal history. Sometimes we choose the same path over and over again, even though it never works out the way we'd like it to, just because it is familiar and there is some comfort in that. Other times, if we are feeling brave or adventurous, we choose the unknown in order that we may have new experiences and possibly redesign our lives with something that works much better.

In today's assignment, you will sit with your journal closed, in your lap if you like, and imagine a door. Wait... don't open it yet. Focus on the door first. What color is it? What kind of handle does it have? Is there a window in the door? A peep-hole? What is the door made of? Is it inviting or menacing or something else?

Now imagine what might be on the other side of the door. Okay you can open it (did it make a sound?). Open your journal and write about what is on the other side of the door. Describe what you see with all of your senses. Put yourself in the scene, walking through the door and interacting with the landscape. What do you do? How do you feel? Excited? Nervous? Scared? Joyous? Did you pass through a doorway going in or a door that took you outside? Notice everything and write it down. Pay attention to details.

Upon completion, reflect:

- How did this go for me?
- What did I learn?
- This brought up something new (what?)

(Record your mood after completing the exercise.)

Part Three
Assignment #9

(Record your mood going into the exercise.)

Your Epitaph

Picture yourself passed on, no longer of this world. Try not to let fear invade this thought. Now picture your friends and loved ones at your funeral or a celebration of the life you lived. Eavesdrop. What would they be saying? Is it what you'd want to hear?

This exercise has two parts. Part One is to record the conversation you might hear at your own funeral. Identify the characters in your life and how they'd remember you.

Part Two is to plan your own ceremony. Write your own epitaph. What do you want to be remembered for? What legacy would you like to leave behind? What might your family and friends do that would truly honor your life? What music would you want played? Who do you want to invite? Do you want to be buried or cremated? Do you want Flowers? Charity? Food? Poetry?

It's your party after all, so you may as well plan it. Or not.

Note: Many people feel a great resistance to this exercise. If this is how you are feeling, write about what that resistance means to you.

Upon completion, reflect:

· How did this go for me?
· What did I learn?
· This brought up something new (what?)

(Record your mood after completing the exercise.)

Part Three
Assignment #10

(Record your mood going into the exercise.)

Feast your Eyes on This

Whenever I ask people to write about their favorite things—what they seek out to comfort themselves—the overwhelming majority of responses are foods.

Food is satisfying in more ways than just filling an empty belly. If presented well, foods can be eye candy, a plethora of aromas; a mixture of hot and cold, sweet and savory, smooth and crunchy. They even make different sounds. Think about the sound of pudding versus the sound of peanuts.

In today's exercise you will lay out a banquet of your favorite foods. Describe each and every detail from the table settings to the lighting. Describe the flavors using words you would not normally use to describe foods. For instance, mashed potatoes might be described as buttered cumulus clouds. The smell of chowder may be akin to sunshine laced with honey.

Challenge your senses with delightful textures. Let your mind swell with anticipation.

Don't be surprised if you raid the refrigerator after you complete this exercise. Bon Apetit!

Upon completion, reflect:

· How did this go for me?
· What did I learn?
· This brought up something new (what?)

(Record your mood after completing the exercise.)

Part Three
Assignment #11

(Record your mood going into the exercise.)

Tiny Windows

Anne Lamott, in her wonderful book, *Bird by Bird*, talks about putting little picture frames around tiny segments of her writing so that she can zone in on one thing without the clutter of everything on the peripheral interfering with the story.

So often we whiz through life seeing the Big Picture but missing what is hiding within the landscape. In this exercise, you will focus on one teensy part of your day. Close your eyes and think back over the past 24 hours. Let your mind's lens zoom in on one frame. Perhaps there was someone standing in line in front of you at the grocery store and you overheard her conversation with the cashier. What did they talk about? What were each of them wearing?

Or maybe as you were walking or driving home from work, something in the scenery caught your eye... something worth capturing here on the page.

Again, use as many senses as possible in your writing. Peek through the peephole and leave an invisible reader hungering for more. You may find that you remember more than you thought you would. Or you may have to make up the parts you don't remember. That's okay too. What is important is that you allow yourself to relax and let the images and feelings come to you. Write about the emotions this piece of your day invoke.

Upon completion, reflect:

· How did this go for me?
· What did I learn?
· This brought up something new (what?)

(Record your mood after completing the exercise.)

Part Three
Assignment #12

(Record your mood going into the exercise.)

Picture This

A picture paints a thousand words. How many times have you heard this sentiment?

However overused, what remains true is that pictures do indeed allow us to paint words. What is most fascinating though, is that the same picture will paint a different set of words for each viewer.

For instance, when I look at a painting of a little boy building a sandcastle, I might tell a story of how this little boy is feeling. Maybe I see his loneliness and the castle as his fortress. Another person might tell the story of how he is thinking about how good the sand feels in his hands and that he is ignoring his mother's call from her blanket further up the beach. And yet another may say that he's not building a castle at all. He found this castle and he is dismantling it because he is angry that his sister gets to play with the one and only bucket.

In this exercise you will choose a picture and paint 1,000 words. That may seem like a lot of words, but trust yourself. You know the story and it is waiting to be told. You can choose a photograph, a picture from a magazine, or a framed piece of art. There doesn't need to be people in the picture. Even a picture of the sky can tell a story.

Remember to use all of your senses. Write as if you are the only one that can see the picture. Describe it in detail so that an invisible reader feels like he or she is in the scene.

Upon completion, reflect:

· How did this go for me?
· What did I learn?
· This brought up something new (what?)

(Record your mood after completing the exercise.)

Part Three
Assignment #13

(Record your mood going into the exercise.)

If These Walls Could Talk

They say that home is where the heart is, but a friend of mine recently shared this quote, "Home is where people understand you." I think this fits for a lot of us.

Our homes are our nests, our resting ground. They are supposed to make us feel safe and comfortable. A home should be a welcome refuge, a sanctuary and a hub of activity, depending upon the time of day.

Home sweet home. Or is it? Was it? In this exercise you will choose a home, either the one you live in now or one from your past, and describe it in detail. Enter the rooms and describe the feeling(s) they emit. How do the floors feel under your feet? Does this home still stand? Are there special memories housed within the plaster? What does it smell like? What ghosts linger there?

Optional Exercise: let the walls talk. Tell your story from the house's point of view. Describe the inhabitants, the furniture, and the mood.

Upon completion, reflect:

· How did this go for me?
· What did I learn?
· This brought up something new (what?)

(Record your mood after completing the exercise.)

Part Three
Assignment #14

(Record your mood going into the exercise.)

Reunion

Have you ever fantasized about having a reunion with someone you've long ago lost? A childhood friend, a former lover, a significant mentor?

In today's exercise you get to have that reunion. Write about it the way you imagine it would be or would like it to be. You can even have a reunion with someone who has died.

As always, offer lots of details. What does he or she look like today? How long has it been? Is there any unfinished business to tend to? Write about that too. Here's an example:

I haven't seen Lili since that last time she left my house after singing me to sleep. She sat on the floor next to my bed with her guitar and sang ever so sweetly.

But today I found her! I was walking along the sidewalk when suddenly I spotted her across the street. I knew it had to be her. Although her wild hair is now streaked with gray, she bore the same freckles, the same way of gazing upward when she walked, as if she were looking for a bird.

"*Lili!*" *I screamed and she looked over at me, puzzled, and then a smile, that familiar smile, spread across her face and she ran towards me. We hugged in the middle of the street, the cars honking as they moved around us. I think we stood there for a full three minutes before went into the coffee shop and sat down for two decade's worth of coffee.*"

Enjoy your reunion.

Upon completion, reflect:

· How did this go for me?
· What did I learn?
· This brought up something new (what?)

(Record your mood after completing the exercise.)

Part Three
Assignment #15

(Record your mood going into the exercise.)

Dream Maker

I recently had a dream about my father in which he came to me to foretell his death and say his good-byes. It was an extraordinary dream and I remember it vividly even now. He was wearing bib overalls, something my conservative father wouldn't be caught dead in, no pun intended.

Dreams can be fascinating, but they're usually only interesting to the person who dreams them. However, dreams can also be a breeding ground for fantastical stories, especially sci-fi and fantasy.

In today's assignment, you will tell a dream from the third person point of view, giving yourself (if you are in the dream) a different name. Tell the dream as you would a story. It can be a recurring dream, a recent dream, or even one that someone else has told you if you don't remember your dreams. If there are parts missing, make them up. Leave out the boring parts and weave the dream into a story that is no longer recognized as a dream.

(Incidentally, my father died between the time I began writing this book and was ready to go to press. I am now even more grateful for his presence in my dreams.)

Upon completion, reflect:

· How did this go for me?
· What did I learn?
· This brought up something new (what?)

(Record your mood after completing the exercise.)

Part Three
Assignment #16

(Record your mood going into the exercise.)

Knock-Knock

Who's there?
Orange
Orange who?
Orange you going to tell me who's on the other side of the door?

Kidding aside, we are who we are as a result of every experience we have had; every person who has touched our life, good and bad. As you move from people to characters in your journal, it is helpful to do a spontaneous mind/heart search just to find out who might be lurking on the other side of the door.

Today I want you to imagine a knock on your door. Without thinking, answer it. Describe who is on the other side, real or fantasy. Why is he or she here? Do you let him or her in? What happens next? Write all the juicy details, as if you were writing a story.

You are.

Upon completion, reflect:

- How did this go for me?
- What did I learn?
- This brought up something new (what?)

(Record your mood after completing the exercise.)

Part Three
Assignment #17

(Record your mood going into the exercise.)

The Book of Life

Imagine your life as a book. Would it be a mystery? A thriller? A sci-fi? A romance? Perhaps even erotica? No? How about a classic piece of literature? A comedy? Maybe a best seller?

If your book were made into a movie, who would play the part of you? Who would the supporting cast be? What would be the theme song?

Today's exercise is to choose a title that most closely resembles your Book of Life. Then, write out the chapter headings that relate to the phases of your story so far. Here is an example:

Finding my Way Home
A Serious Comedy by Eldonna Bouton

1. A Parsonage and a Pear Tree
2. In Sickness and in More Sickness
3. Playing House with my Boyfriend
4. Whoops I'm Pregnant
5. Whoops I Married an Alcoholic
6. Whoops I Married Another Alcoholic

All right, lets get going on your Book of Life. Page one...

Upon completion, reflect:

· How did this go for me?
· What did I learn?
· This brought up something new (what?)

(Record your mood after completing the exercise.)

Part Three
Assignment #18

(Record your mood going into the exercise.)

The Second Book of Life

In the last exercise you titled the book of your life and wrote chapter headings. But your life isn't finished yet, so how could your book be complete? Wouldn't it be wonderful if we could write the ending we'd like? Wait... we can!

In this exercise you will finish the book as if you have lived out your life the way you would like. NOT how you necessarily think it will turn out, but the life you dream of living. The one where you get to "Choose Your Own Adventure" just like in those juvenile mystery books.

Write, "Part Two" after Assignment #17 and then begin authoring the rest of the chapters of your Book of Life, as you would like it to be. As a strong believer in intention and manifestation, I am going to ask you to wait until you can do this exercise mindfully. You may be surprised at what can happen when you dream upon the page.

Like a happy ending, for starters.

Note: You will <u>not</u> jinx yourself.

Upon completion, reflect:

· How did this go for me?
· What did I learn?
· This brought up something new (what?)

(Record your mood after completing the exercise.)

Part Three
Assignment #19

(Record your mood going into the exercise.)

If I Were King

I apologize for the gender bias, but when we get into the exercise, the sex of the person wearing the crown will become insignificant.

How many times have you wished you were the one making all the decisions that directly (or indirectly) affect you? For instance, in my sweet little town a beautiful meadow is being turned into Big Box stores. I'm terribly disappointed. Being the tree-hugger type, I wish I could have been the one casting the deciding vote on whether to allow the ordinance change.

On a more personal level, there are things I can't do in my own home (such as leave my dishes sit overnight) because in a household of more than one, we each have to respect each other's comfort levels. But...

If I were queen, things would change. Around here and around the world. Children and animals would have more rights than greedy corporations. People would be required to respect each other. And when I'm tired I would leave my dishes until morning.

How about you? Today write "If I were king/queen..." and start in on your decrees. Start small with things like "I would have more of the closet space" and work your way up to "There would be no HMO's." Have fun, yet notice which things are truly in your power to change and which things you might at least throw a little more of your activist self into.

Upon completion, reflect:

· How did this go for me?
· What did I learn?
· This brought up something new (what?)

(Record your mood after completing the exercise.)

Part Three
Assignment #20

(Record your mood going into the exercise.)

Microcosmos

There is a scene in the movie "Microcosmos" where two snails are filmed at eye level as they approach each other for eventual copulation. It is one of the sexiest love scenes I have ever witnessed. It is set to music and these two snails–I swear to you they embrace–are shown in all their deliciously slimy glory. It is a sight to behold.

It also reminds me of how often we rush through life, not slowing down enough to savor each tiny moment.

Today observe something small but intricate; complicated. Like an anthill or a spider spinning a web or, if you're lucky, snails making love. Then write about it so that you never forget what you have been privileged to witness.

(If you've never seen Microcosmos, rent it! No words, just an hour of life among the kingdom of those who exist under leaves and on the forest floor set to beautiful music. You will be blessed as a guest among the finest creatures among us.)

Upon completion, reflect:

· How did this go for me?
· What did I learn?
· This brought up something new (what?)

(Record your mood after completing the exercise.)

Part Three
Assignment #21

(Record your mood going into the exercise.)

Baby Talk

Have you ever wondered what's going through an infant's head as he or she looks at you, wide-eyed and innocent? Perhaps you've had children of your own and often wished you could understand the meaning of their cries. Or, as a parent, you may wish you could tell your newborn all about life and love and why you chose to bring them into the world.

Just for a moment, imagine you are in your mother's arms. You were born only moments ago. Imagine that you have been gifted with the ability to speak. What do you and your mother talk about?

Write a dialogue between you and your mother. Ask what you've always wished you could have asked. Listen to what she says.

You can take this assignment another step by having your mother hand you to your father and repeating the exercise.

Be sure to make it a two-way conversation.

Upon completion, reflect:

· How did this go for me?
· What did I learn?
· This brought up something new (what?)

(Record your mood after completing the exercise.)

Part Three
Assignment #22

(Record your mood going into the exercise.)

These Shoes Were Made for Walkin'

As a bodyworker, I see a lot of feet. Sometimes people screw up their faces and say, "Ew! How can you stand to rub all those icky feet?"

I tell them that it's an honor, and truly it is. Every time I hold a new foot in my hand, I wonder about where it has been on this journey so far. I am especially awed when I hold in my hand the foot of one of my elderly clients. Sometimes I try to imagine all the places it has been, floors it has walked, miles it has logged.

In today's exercise you're not going to write about feet. Did I fool you? Well, actually we're going to write about shoes.

Describe a pair of shoes you might find at the thrift shop. Let them tell their story. What of their owner(s) and the lives they have shared? Walk a mile (or more) in these shoes.

Upon completion, reflect:

- How did this go for me?
- What did I learn?
- This brought up something new (what?)

(Record your mood after completing the exercise.)

Part Three
Assignment #23

(Record your mood going into the exercise.)

Shadow Box

When my husband and I moved to California from Michigan in 1997, we noticed things turning up missing. After about six months we realized that the last box we had packed, the one in which we just sort of threw whatever was left lying around, had somehow not made the trip. We're still not sure if it was left behind or if the movers got it mixed up with someone else's stuff. But every now and then when we can't find something, one of us will say, "Oh. It must have been in the box."

Sometimes it's fun to imagine the person who ended up with our box trying to figure out what kind of people we are. There wasn't anything terribly valuable inside, but it did contain stuff that might tell a lot about us.

Write about discovering a box. Where do you find it? Is it delivered to you? Do you hesitate or immediately open it? Describe the contents. What do the box and its contents reveal about the person who left it behind (or sent it)?

Upon completion, reflect:

- How did this go for me?
- What did I learn?
- This brought up something new (what?)

(Record your mood after completing the exercise.)

Part Three
Assignment #24

(Record your mood going into the exercise.)

No Holding Back

This is a test. Just how willing are you to submit to your creative spirit? Something tells me there is (at least) one thing you have always avoided writing about. Perhaps you think it's too messy, too erotic, or there is shame attached to it. Maybe you think it's too silly or not good enough.

Today you will write what you have not written. Let out all the stops. Write any words you want to and in any style. If you have always wanted to write a poem but told yourself you are not a poet, write it. If you have a juicy bit of erotica lounging in your inner bedroom (or elsewhere), write about it. If you just want to write in circles on the page, go ahead. Sometimes it helps to start with, "I will not write ." or "I can't write ."

You have just been handed "creative license." Take your pen for a drive!

Upon completion, reflect:

· How did this go for me?
· What did I learn?
· This brought up something new (what?)

(Record your mood after completing the exercise.)

Part Three
Assignment #25

(Record your mood going into the exercise.)

The Writer Speaks

We are all drawn to the page for different reasons. Most journal writers begin as "cathartic writers," spewing their angst like fire out of their pens.

Once they reach a level of therapeutic release, many journalers will then become more and more creative in their journals. For whatever reason, they keep coming back to the page.

So now it is time to ask yourself, "Am I content to continue with a writer's journal filled with exploratory writing or do I want to take my writing to the next level? If so, what level? Am I interested in becoming a published writer? If so, what genre?"

In this final assignment, describe your writing goals. Continue to reap the harvest of seeds planted in your writer's journal, but consider the possibility that you have sparked your muse and she begs for more. Consider the possibility that there *is* more.

Unless of course for now, this is enough. In any case, keep your heart open and your pen ready. And for crying out loud, write.

Upon completion, reflect:

· How did this go for me?
· What did I learn?
· This brought up something new (what?)

(Record your mood after completing the exercise.)

Bibliography of Journaling Books

Adams, Kathleen, *Journal to the Self: Twenty-Two Paths to Personal Growth*, Warner Books, 1990.

Adams, Kathleen, *The Way of the Journal: A Journal Therapy Workbook for Healing*, Luthersville: Sidran Press, 1993.

Adams, Kathleen, *The Write Way To Wellness*, 1999.

Aftel, Mandy, *The Story of Your Life: Becoming the Author of Your Experience*, Simon & Schuster, 1996.

Albert, Susan Wittig, *Writing From Life: Telling Your Soul's Story*, Tarcher, 1996.

Aldrich, Anne Hazard, *Notes from Myself: A Guide to Creative Journal Writing*, Carroll & Graf, 1998.

Aronie, Nancy Slonim, *Writing From the Heart, Tapping the Power of your Inner Voice*, Hyperion, 1998.

Baldwin, Christina, *Life's Companion: Journal-Writing as a Spiritual Quest*, Bantam, 1990.

Baldwin, Christina, *One to One: Self-Understanding Through Journal Writing*, M. Evans and Company, 1977.

Barrington, Judith, *Writing the Memoir: From Truth to Art*, The Eighth Mountain Press, 1996.

Bernays, Anne & Painter, Pamela, *What If? Writing Exercises for Fiction Writers*, Harper Perrenial, 1991.

Borkin, Susan, *Writing From the Inside Out*, Center for Personal Growth, 1995.

Bouton, Eldonna Edwards, *Loose Ends, A Journaling Tool for Tying up the Incomplete Details of Your Life and Heart*, Whole Heart Publications, 1999.

Bouton, Eldonna Edwards, *Journaling from the Heart: A Workshop in Three Parts*, Whole Heart Publications, 2000.

Bouton, Eldonna Edwards, *Write in this Book! An Interactive Writer's Journal*, Whole Heart Publications, 2001.

Bouton, Eldonna Edwards, *Write Away: A Journal Writing Toolkit*, Whole Heart Publications, 2000.

Breathnach, Sara Ban, *Simple Abundance (series)*, Warner Books, 1996+.

Brown, Rita Mae, *Starting from Scratch, A Different Kind of Writer's Manual*, Bantam, 1989.

Cameron, Julia, *The Artist's Way*, Tarcher/Putnam, 1992.

Cameron, Julia, *The Right to Write*, Tarcher/Putnam, 1999.

Cameron, Julia, *Vein of Gold*, Tarcher Putnam, 1997.

Cappachione, Lucia, *The Creative Journal: The Art of Finding Yourself*, Swallow,press, 1979.

Cerwinske, Laura, *Writing as a Healing Art*, Perigree, 1999.

Chapman, Joyce, *Journaling for Joy: Writing Your Way to Personal Growth and Freedom*, Newcastle Publishing, 1991.

Coleman, Vernon, *Know Yourself: 940 Questions That Uncover the Real You*, Fawcett Crest, 1989.

Edelstein, Scott, *The No-Experience Writer's Course*, Scarborough House, 1990.

Field, Joanna, *A Life of One's Own*, Tarcher, 1981/1936.

Forrest, Jan, *Coming Home to Ourselves, A Woman's Journey to Wholeness*, Heart to Heart Productions, 1998.

Friedman, Bonnie, *Writing Past Dark: Envy, Fear, Distraction, and Other Dilemmas in the Writer's Life*, HarperPerenniel, 1993.

Goldberg, Natalie, *Writing Down the Bones: Freeing the Writer Within*, Shambhala, 1986.

McDonnell, Jane Taylor. *Living to Tell the Tale: A Guide to Writing Memoir*, New York: Penguin, 1998.

Nelson, G. Lynn, *Writing and Being*, Innisfree Press, 1994.

Metzger, Deena. *Writing For Your Life: A Guide and Companion to the Inner Worlds*, HarperSanFrancisco, 1992.

Miller, James E., *The Rewarding Practice of Journal Writing*, Willowgreen, 1998.

Newman, Leslea. *Writing from the Heart, Inspiration and Exercises for Women who want to Write*, The Crossing Press, 1993.

Offner, Rose. *Journal to the Soul: The Art of Sacred Journal Keeping*, Gibbs Smith Publisher, 1996.

Progoff, Ira. *At a Journal Workshop: The Basic Text and Guide for Using the Intensive Journal*, Dialogue House Library, 1975.

Progoff, Ira. *Life Study: Experiencing Creative Lives by the Intensive Journal Method*, Dialogue House Library, 1983.

Rainer, Tristine. *The New Diary: How to Use a Journal for Self-Guidance and Expanded Creativity*, Tarcher, 1978.

Rainer, Tristine. *Your Life as Story: Writing the New Autobiography*, Tarcher, 1997.

Rico, Gabriele. *Pain and Possibility*, Tarcher, 1991.

Sark. *Sark's Journal and Play Book*, Celestial Arts, 1996.

Shiwy, Marlene A. *A Voice of Her Own: Women and the Journal-Writing Journey*, 1996.

Snow, Kimberly. *Writing Yourself Home, A Woman's Guided Journey of Self-Discovery*, Conari Press, 1989.

Stanek, Lou Willett, Ph. D. *Writing Your Life, Putting Your Past on Paper*, Avon, 1996.

Ueland, Brenda. *If You Want to Write, A Book about Independence and Spirit*, Gray Wolf Press, 1984.

About the Author

Eldonna Edwards Bouton has published inspirational nonfiction as well as essays, humor and fiction. She is the author of *Loose Ends: A Journaling Tool for Tying up the Incomplete Details of your Life and Heart* (Whole Heart Publications, 1999) and *Write Away: A Journal Writing Tool Kit* (Whole Heart Publications, 1999.) *Write in this Book! An Interactive Writer's Journal*, is scheduled for publication in 2001.

She currently offers " *Journaling from the Heart™*" workshops and seminars nationally, and on the Central California Coast where she resides. To find out more about *Journaling from the Heart* workshops, visit http://www.whole-heart.com.

The Author can be reached in care of Whole Heart Publications, P. O. Box 14358, San Luis Obispo, CA 93406-4358 or by e-mail at author@whole-heart.com.

Order Form for Fax and Snail Mail Orders

Please send _____copies of *Loose Ends, A Journaling Tool for Tying up the Incomplete Details of your Life and Heart* at $13.95. ea.
Please send _____ copies of *Journaling from the Heart* at $14.95 ea.
Please send _____ copies of *Write Away Booklet* at $6.95 ea.

Shipping for books is $3.20 for first book and $1.50 each additional book. Shipping is included in booklet price.

Bill to ___Visa _____ MasterCard

(California residents add 7.5% sales tax) for a total of $ _____

Card # _____

Expiration _____ Name on card: _____

Ship to: _____

City_____ State_____

Zip_____ Phone_____ E-mail _____

Do you want the author to sign your copy? _____

Fax this page to 805-543-8640.
OR:

Mail this form with your check or money order to: Whole Heart Publications, PO Box 14358, San Luis Obispo, CA, 93406-4358. You can also order on the web at http://www.whole-heart.com. Or ask your bookstore to order if they don't have it.